Marley gets comfortable in our backyard shortly after we brought him home.

Marley

Marley on his first night at home,
crying to get out of his box.

Grogan's Majestic Marley of Churchill did have a
regal bearing—when he wasn't chasing his tail.

Sun, sand, surf—and his master, too.
Life is good!

Have bowl, will travel! Even as a puppy, Marley loved sloshing water all over the house.

Marley exploring the garage on his first day home.

"Ah, nothing like a nice refreshing drink of saltwater."

"Can you people please speak in dog?"

In hot southern Florida, Marley loved to stretch out on the cool tile floor.

Marley peers in from outside on the pool deck.

Marley relaxing on Dog Beach minutes before throwing up in the water.

This is our last photo of him, taken days before we said our final good-byes.

In his last year, Marley mostly slept.

Marley
A Dog Like No Other

사전없이 원서읽기 **말리와 나**

초판 1쇄 인쇄 2010년 8월 23일
초판 1쇄 발행 2010년 8월 28일

지은이 존 그로건 **해설** 황소연
기획 및 책임편집 홍성은 **교정·교열** 김수진
디자인 남다희 **삽화** 고상미
마케팅 손정선, 손지훈 **경영지원** 마하선
펴낸이 조치영 **펴낸곳** 스크린영어사

서울특별시 관악구 대학동 1514번지
TEL (02) 887-8416
FAX (02) 887-8591
http://www.screenplay.co.kr

등록일자 1997년 7월 9일
등록번호 제16-1495

ISBN 978-89-6415-026-9   13740

✽ 잘못된 책은 서점에서 바꾸어 드립니다.

Marley: A Dog Like No Other
Copyright © 2007 by John Grogan
All rights reserved

English text with Korean annotation copyright © 2010 by Screen English Publishing Co.
English text with Korean annotation rights arranged with DeFiore and Company through EYA

이 책의 한국어 주석판 저작권은 EYA(Eric Yang Agency)를 통한 DeFiore and Company와의 독점 계약으로 스크린영어사가 소유합니다. 저작권법에 의하여 한국 내에서 보호를 받는 저작물이므로 무단전재와 복제를 금합니다.

Cover art © 2010 Twentieth Century Fox Film Corporation. All Rights Reserved

Marley
A Dog Like No Other

John Grogan

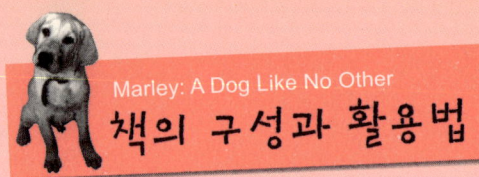

책의 구성과 활용법

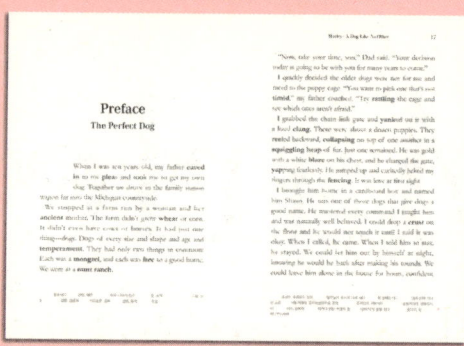

사전없이 원서읽기

사전없이 원서를 읽을 수 있도록 본문에서 가장 중요하고 어려운 단어와 표현만 골라서, 해당 문장에서 사용된 뜻과 기본적인 뜻을 소개한다. 모르는 어휘만 확인하도록 본문 하단에 주석을 달아놓았다.

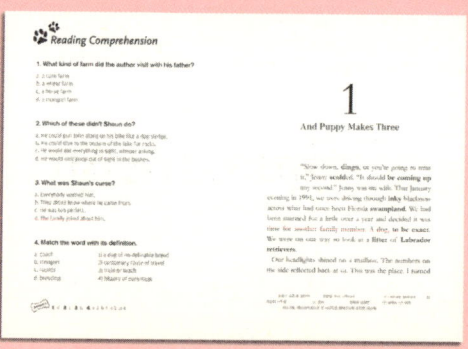

Reading Comprehension

한 챕터를 읽고 나서 자신이 본문 내용을 얼마나 이해했는지 간단한 연습문제를 통해 확인한다.

챕터별 줄거리

본문을 읽고 나서 한글 줄거리를 보고 확인하거나, 영화를 보지 않은 사람은 한글 줄거리를 미리 한번 보고 나서 원서를 읽는 것도 독해에 좀 더 도움이 될 수 있다.

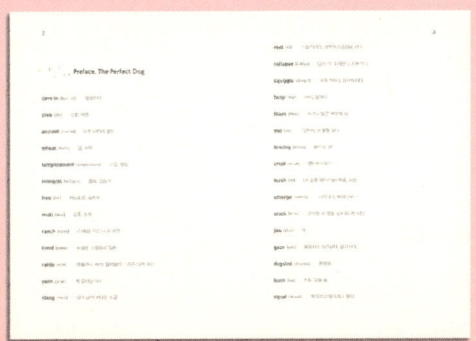

Vocabulary Plus

본문에 주석으로 달린 어휘들을 모아 좀 더 자세한 의미와 영영해석을 확인한다. 스크린영어사 공식 카페를 통해서 내려받을 수 있다.

Contents

Preface
The Perfect Dog — 8

Chapter 1
And Puppy Makes Three — 13

Chapter 2
Homeward Bound — 20

Chapter 3
Mr. Wiggles — 28

Chapter 4
Master and Beast — 36

Chapter 5
A Battle of Wills — 45

Chapter 6
The Great Escape — 63

Chapter 7
The Things He Ate — 69

Chapter 8
The Dog's Got to Go — 82

Chapter 9
The Final Round — 93

Chapter 10
The Audition — 100

Chapter 11
Take Two — 115

Chapter 12
Jail Break 120

Chapter 13
Dinner Time! 131

Chapter 14
Lightning Strikes 140

Chapter 15
Dog Beach 147

Chapter 16
A Northbound Plane 161

Chapter 17
In the Land of Pencils 170

Chapter 18
Poultry on Parade 183

Chapter 19
The Potty Room 198

Chapter 20
Beating the Odds 214

Chapter 21
Borrowed Time 226

Chapter 22
The Big Meadow 237

Chapter 23
Beneath the Cherry Trees 250

Chapter 24
Lucky 261

Chapter Synopsis 267

Preface
The Perfect Dog

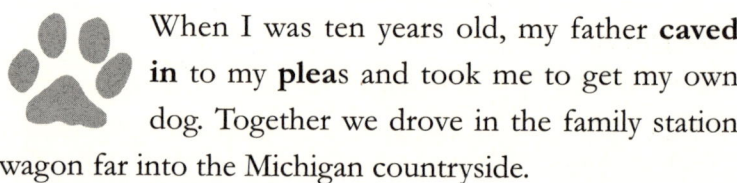When I was ten years old, my father **caved in** to my **plea**s and took me to get my own dog. Together we drove in the family station wagon far into the Michigan countryside.

We stopped at a farm run by a woman and her **ancient** mother. The farm didn't grow **wheat** or corn. It didn't even have cows or horses. It had just one thing—dogs. Dogs of every size and shape and age and **temperament**. They had only two things in common: Each was a **mongrel**, and each was **free** to a good home. We were at a **mutt ranch**.

cave in 항복하다 plea 간청, 애원 ancient 아주 나이가 많은 wheat 밀, 소맥 temperament 기질, 성질 mongrel 잡종, 잡종개 free 자유로운, 공짜의 mutt 잡종, 똥개 ranch 목장

"Now, take your time, son," Dad said. "Your decision today is going to be with you for many years to come."

I quickly decided the older dogs were not for me and raced to the puppy cage. "You want to pick one that's not **timid**," my father coached. "Try **rattling** the cage and see which ones aren't afraid."

I grabbed the chain-link gate and **yank**ed on it with a loud **clang**. There were about a dozen puppies. They **reel**ed backward, **collapsing** on top of one another in a **squiggling heap** of fur. Just one remained. He was gold with a white **blaze** on his chest, and he charged the gate, **yap**ping fearlessly. He jumped up and excitedly licked my fingers through the **fencing**. It was love at first sight.

I brought him home in a cardboard box and named him Shaun. He was one of those dogs that give dogs a good name. He mastered every command I taught him and was naturally well behaved. I could drop a **crust** on the floor and he would not touch it until I said it was okay. When I called, he came. When I told him to stay, he stayed. We could let him out by himself at night, knowing he would be back after making his rounds. We could leave him alone in the house for hours, confident

---

timid 소심한, 수줍음이 많은　rattle 덜컥덜컥 소리가 나게 하다　yank 홱 잡아당기다　clang (금속성의) 커다란 소음　reel 비틀거리다, 갈지자걸음으로 걷다　collapse 주저앉다, 쓰러지다　squiggle 꿈틀거리다, 몸부림치다　heap 더미, 덩어리　blaze 희거나 밝은 색깔의 점　yap (강아지가) 왈왈 짖다　fencing 울타리, 담　crust (빵) 부스러기

that he wouldn't have an accident or disturb a thing. He raced cars without chasing them and walked beside me without a **leash**. He could dive to the bottom of our lake and **emerge** with rocks so big they sometimes got **stuck** in his **jaw**s. He loved riding in the car. He'd sit quietly in the backseat beside me on family road trips, happy to **gaze** out the window as the world zoomed by.

Best of all, I trained Shaun to pull me through the neighborhood **dogsled**-style as I sat on my bicycle. My friends jealously watched as he carefully guided me down the street, never leading me into trouble.

Shaun even had the good manners to back himself into the **bush**es before **squat**ting to **poop**. With his rear end hidden away, only his head **peer**ed out. Our lawn was safe for bare feet.

Relatives would visit for the weekend and return home determined to buy a dog of their own. They were that impressed with Shaun. Actually, I called him "Saint Shaun." The saint part was a family joke, but we almost believed it.

Shaun had been born with a **curse**—no one knew who his parents were. Because his **breeding** was unknown, he

leash (개 등을 매어두는) 목줄, 사슬   emerge 나타나다, 빠져나오다   stuck (움직일 수 없을 정도로) 꽉 끼인
jaw 턱   gaze 물끄러미 바라보다, 응시하다   dogsled 개썰매   bush 관목, 덤불 숲   squat 쪼그리고/웅크리고
앉다   poop 똥을 싸다   peer 뚫어지게 보다, 응시하다   curse 불운   breeding 혈통, 가계

was one of the tens of thousands of unwanted dogs in America. Yet **by some stroke of good luck**, he became wanted. He came into my life and I came into his. And he gave me the childhood every kid deserves.

Saint Shaun of my childhood. He was a perfect dog. At least that is how I will always remember him. It was Shaun who set the standard by which I would judge all other dogs to come.

by a stroke of good luck 운이 좋아서

Reading Comprehension

1. What kind of farm did the author visit with his father?

a. a corn farm
b. a wheat farm
c. a horse farm
d. a mongrel farm

2. Which of these didn't Shaun do?

a. He could pull John along on his bike like a dog sledge.
b. He could dive to the bottom of the lake for rocks.
c. He would eat everything in sight, without asking.
d. He would only poop out of sight in the bushes.

3. What was Shaun's curse?

a. Everybody wanted him.
b. Anyone didn't know where he came from.
c. He was too perfect.
d. The family joked about him.

4. Match the word with its definition.

a. coach   1) a dog of no definable breed
b. mongrel   2) customary route of travel
c. rounds   3) train or teach
d. breeding   4) history of parentage

Answers: **1.** d **2.** c **3.** b **4.** a-3, b-1, c-2, d-4

1

And Puppy Makes Three

"Slow down, **dingo**, or you're going to miss it," Jenny **scold**ed. "It should **be coming up** any second." Jenny was my wife. That January evening in 1991, we were driving through **inky** blackness across what had once been Florida **swampland**. We had been married for a little over a year and decided it was time for another family member. A dog, **to be exact**. We were on our way to look at a **litter** of **Labrador retrievers**.

Our headlights shined on a mailbox. The numbers on the side reflected back at us. This was the place. I turned

---

dingo 호주산 토종개, 얼간이 scold 핀잔을 주다, 나무라다 be coming up 곧 나타나다, 일어나다 inky 칠흑같이 어두운 swampland 늪, 습지 to be exact 정확히 말하면 litter (한 배에서 난) 새끼 Labrador retriever 래브라도 리트리버(총으로 쏜 사냥감을 물어오도록 훈련된 사냥개)

up a **gravel** drive that led into a large wooded **property**. There was a pond in front of the house and a small **barn** out back. At the door, a woman named Lori greeted us, with a big, calm yellow Labrador retriever by her side.

"This is Lily, the proud mama," Lori said. Lily's stomach was still **swollen** even though she'd given birth five weeks before.

Jenny and I **got on our knees**, and Lily happily accepted our affection. She was just what we pictured a Lab would be—sweet natured, **affectionate**, calm, and beautiful.

"Where's the father?" I asked.

"Oh," the woman said, hesitating for just a **fraction** of a second. "Sammy Boy? He's around here somewhere." She quickly added, "I imagine you're **dying to see** the puppies."

Lori led us through the kitchen into a **utility room**. The puppies **stumble**d all over one another as they rushed to check out the strangers.

Jenny **gasp**ed. "I don't think I've ever seen anything so cute in my life," she said.

The litter consisted of five females and four males.

---

gravel 자갈 property 소유한 건물과 땅 barn 헛간, 광, 외양간 swollen 부풀어 오른, 부은 get on one's knee 무릎을 꿇고 앉다 affectionate 다정한 fraction 아주 조금 be dying to do 몹시(간절히) 하고 싶어하다 utility room 다용도실 stumble 발부리가 걸리다, 휘청거리다 gasp (놀라서) 헉 숨을 들이마시다, 가쁜 숨을 쉬다

Lori was asking $400 for the females and $375 for the males. One of the males seemed particularly **smitten with** us. He was the **goofiest** of the group and charged into us. **Somersault**ing into our laps, he **clawed his way** up our shirts to lick our faces. He **gnaw**ed on our fingers with surprisingly sharp baby teeth and **stomp**ed **clumsy** circles around us on giant paws that were way too big for the rest of his body.

"That one there you can have for three hundred fifty dollars," Lori said.

"Aw, honey," Jenny **coo**ed. "The little guy's on **clearance**!"

I had to admit he was pretty **darn adorable**. **Frisky**, too. Before I realized what he was up to, the **rascal** had chewed off half my watchband.

"We have to do the scare test," I said. I had told Jenny the story many times of picking out Saint Shaun when I was a boy. Sitting in this heap of **pup**s, she **rolled her eyes at** me. "Seriously," I said. "It works."

I stood up and turned away from the puppies. Then I swung quickly back around, taking a sudden step toward them. I stomped my foot and barked out, "Hey!"

---

smitten with 홀딱 반한 goofy 어리버리한, 덜 떨어진 somersault 공중제비를 돌다 claw one's way (양손을) 휘저으며 나아가다 gnaw 잘근잘근 씹다 stomp (쿵쿵거리며) 걷다, 발을 구르다 clumsy 서투른, 어설픈, (선이) 일그러진, 비대칭의 coo 정답게 소곤거리다 clearance 떨이, 세일 darn 매우, 대단히 adorable 매우 사랑스러운/귀여운 frisky 장난치기 좋아하는, 활달한 rascal 장난꾸러기, 악당 pup 강아지 roll one's eyes at 눈알을 굴려 불신이나 짜증을 표시하다

I didn't seem to scare any of them. But only one **plunge**d forward to meet the **assault head-on**. It was Clearance Dog. He **plow**ed full **steam** into me, **throwing a cross-body block** across my ankles. Then he **pounce**d at my shoelaces as though he was convinced they were dangerous enemies that needed to be destroyed.

"I think it's fate," Jenny said.

"Ya think?" I said. I **scoop**ed him up and held him in one hand in front of my face, studying his **mug**. He looked at me with heart-melting brown eyes and then **nibble**d my nose. I **plop**ped him into Jenny's arms, where he did the same to her. "He certainly seems to like us," I said.

Clearance Dog was ours. We wrote Lori a check, and she told us we could return to take the dog home with us in three weeks, when he was eight weeks old. We thanked her, gave Lily one last **pat**, and said good-bye.

Walking to the car, I threw my arm around Jenny's shoulder and pulled her tight to me. "Can you believe it?" I said. "We actually got our dog!"

Just as we were reaching the car, we heard a **commotion** coming from the woods. Something was

---

plunge 뛰어들다, 돌진하다   assault 맹공, 돌격   head-on 정면으로   plow 쏟아붓다   steam 에너지, 힘
throw a cross-body block 위에서 덮쳐서 십자 모양으로 내리누르다   pounce 와락 덤벼들다, 달려들다
scoop 들어 올리다   mug 얼굴, 얼간이   nibble (잘근잘근) 씹다   plop (톡) 떨어뜨리다   pat (톡톡) 두드리기,
쓰다듬기   commotion 소동, 소란

crashing through the **brush**—and breathing very heavily. It sounded like a creature from a horror film. And it was coming our way. We froze, staring into the darkness. The sound grew louder and closer. Then **in a flash** the thing **burst** into the clearing and came **charging** in our direction, a yellow **blur**. A very *big* yellow blur. As it **gallop**ed past, without stopping or noticing us, we could see it was a large Labrador retriever. But it was nothing like sweet Lily. This one was **soak**ing wet and covered up to its belly in mud and **burr**s. Its tongue hung out wildly to one side. **Froth** flew off its **jowl**s as it **barrel**ed past. I **detect**ed an odd, slightly crazed, yet somehow joyous gaze in its eyes. It was as though this animal had just seen a ghost—and couldn't possibly be more thrilled about it.

Then, with the **roar** of a **stampeding herd** of buffalo, it was gone, around the back of the house and out of sight. Jenny let out a little gasp.

"I think," I said, a slight **queasiness** rising in my **gut**, "we just met Dad."

---

crash 소란을 피우다 brush 덤불 in a flash 순식간에 burst 갑자기 나타나다 charge 돌격하다, 돌진하다 blur 흐릿한 것 gallop 질주하다 soak (흠뻑) 젖다 burr 가시 돋친 씨앗/열매 froth 거품 덩어리 jowl 아래턱 barrel 휙 지나가다, 질주하다 detect 간파하다, 감지하다 roar (우르릉 쿵쾅거리는) 소음 stampede (떼를 지어) 우르르 달아나다 herd 무리, 떼 queasiness 속이 메스껍거나 울렁거리는 느낌 gut 배, 속

Reading Comprehension

1. What test was used to pick the right dog?

a. a cute test to see which dog is the cutest
b. a physical test to see which dog is the most active
c. a scare test to see which dog is the bravest
d. an eating test to see which dog will eat John's watch

2. Why was the puppy Jenny and John chose called Clearance Dog?

a. He was the last male dog.
b. He was offered at a cheaper sale price.
c. He was good at clearing space in the room.
d. The owner wanted to get rid of him.

3. Match the description which best suits each dog.

a. Lily (Mom)   1) goofy, clumsy and adorable
b. Clearance Dog   2) wild, crazy and joyous
c. Sammy (Dad)   3) sweet, calm and beautiful

4. How did Jenny and John feel about their purchase after seeing Clearance Dog's father?

a. surprised and nervous
b. excited and impressed
c. regretful and sorry
d. angry and scared

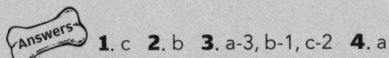

1. c **2.** b **3.** a-3, b-1, c-2 **4.** a

2

Homeward Bound

When it was time to bring the dog home, Jenny was at Disney World with her sister's family, so I picked him up by myself.

Lori brought out my new dog from the back of the house. I gasped. The tiny, **fuzzy** puppy we had picked out three weeks earlier had more than doubled in size. He came barreling at me and ran head first into my ankles. He collapsed in a pile at my feet and rolled onto his back with his paws in the air. I hoped it was his way of telling me I was the boss.

Lori must have sensed my shock. "He's a growing boy,

homeward bound 집으로 향하는   fuzzy (털이) 복슬복슬한

isn't he?" she said cheerily. "You should see him **pack away** the **puppy chow**!"

I leaned down and rubbed his belly. "Ready to go home, Marley?" I asked. That's what Jenny and I had decided to name him—after Bob Marley, our favorite reggae musician. It felt right.

I used beach towels to make a cozy nest for him on the passenger seat of the car. I set him down in it. But I was barely out of the driveway when he began **squirm**ing and **wiggling** his way out of the towels. He **bellycrawl**ed in my direction across the seat, **whimper**ing.

At the center **console**, Marley ran into a problem. There he was, **hind legs** hanging over the passenger side of the console and front legs hanging over the driver's side. In the middle, his stomach was firmly beached on the emergency brake. His little legs were going in all directions, clawing at the air. He wiggled and rocked and **sway**ed, but he was grounded like a **freighter** on a **sandbar**.

I reached over and ran my hand down his back. That made him squiggle even more. His hind paws desperately tried to dig into the carpeted **hump** between the two

---

pack away 먹어 치우다 **puppy chow** 개 사료 **squirm** 꿈틀거리다, 몸부림치다 **wiggle** 몸부림치다 **bellycrawl** 배를 땅에 끌며 기어오다 **whimper** 낑낑거리다, 흐느껴 울다 **console** (자동차) 콘솔 박스 **hind legs** 동물의 뒷다리 **sway** 흔들리다 **freighter** (화물) 수송기 **sandbar** (좁고 긴) 모래사장 **hump** (바닥 등의) 솟아오른 것, (낙타 등의) 혹

seats. Slowly he began working his **hindquarter**s into the air, his butt rising up, up, until the law of **gravity** finally **kicked in**. He slid head first down the other side of the console, somersaulting onto the floor at my feet and **flip**ping onto his back. From there he easily **scramble**d up into my lap.

Man, was he happy—desperately happy! He **quake**d with joy as he **burrow**ed his head into my stomach and nibbled the buttons of my shirt. His tail **slap**ped a steady beat on the **steering wheel**.

I found I could change the tempo of his **wag**ging by touching him. When I had both hands on the wheel, his tail beat three thumps per second. *Thump. Thump. Thump.* If I pressed one finger against the top of his head, the rhythm jumped from a slow waltz to a lively bossa nova. *Thump-thump-thump-thump-thump-thump!* Two fingers and it jumped up to a mambo. *Thump-thumpa-thump-thump-thumpa-thump!* And when I **cupped my** entire **hand** over his head and massaged my fingers into his **scalp**, the beat exploded into a machine-gun, **rapid-fire** samba. *Thumpthumpthumpthumpthump thumpthumpthump!*

hindquarter (네발 짐승의) 엉덩이와 뒷다리   gravity 중력   kick in 작용하다   flip 발랑 뒤집히다, 뒤집다
scramble 허우적대며 나아가다   quake (몸을) 부르르 떨다, 전율하다   burrow 파고들다   slap 찰싹 때리다
steering wheel 운전대   wag (꼬리를) 흔들다   thump (때릴 때 나는) 쿵 소리, 탁 소리   cup one's hand 손을 오므리다   scalp 머릿가죽, 두피   rapid-fire 쏜살 같은, 대단히 빠른

"Wow! You've got rhythm!" I told him. "You really are a reggae dog."

When we got home, I led him inside and **unhook**ed his leash. He began **sniff**ing and didn't stop until he had sniffed every square inch of the place. Then he sat back and looked up at me with his head **cock**ed as if he were saying, "Cool house, but where are my brothers and sisters?"

The reality of his new life didn't really **hit** him until bedtime. I had set up his sleeping **quarter**s in the one-car garage attached to the side of the house. The room was dry and comfortable, and it had a rear door that led out into the fenced backyard. With its concrete floor and walls, it was **virtually indestructible**. "Marley," I said cheerfully, leading him out there, "this is your room."

I had **scatter**ed chew toys around, laid newspapers down in the middle of the floor, filled a bowl with water, and made a bed out of a cardboard box lined with an old **bedspread**.

"And here is where you'll be sleeping," I said, and lowered him into the box. He was used to sleeping in a box, but had always shared it with his **siblings**. Now he

---

unhook 풀다, 끄르다   sniff 킁킁거리며 냄새를 맡다   cock 쫑긋 세우다, 곧추서다   hit 타격을 입히다
quarter 숙소, 보금자리   virtually 사실상   indestructible 파괴할 수 없는   scatter 흩어놓다, 어지럽히다
bedspread 침대 덮개   siblings 형제·자매

paced the **perimeter** of the box and sadly looked up at me. As a test, I stepped back into the house and closed the door. I stood and listened. At first nothing. Then a slight, barely **audible** whimper. And then **full-fledged** crying. It sounded like someone was in there **torturing** him.

I opened the door, and as soon as he saw me he stopped. I reached in and **pet**ted him for a couple of minutes. Then I left again. Standing on the other side of the door, I began to count. One, two, three . . . he made it seven seconds before the **yip**s and cries began again. We repeated the exercise several times. Each time it was the same.

I was tired and decided it was time for him to cry himself to sleep. I left the garage light on for him, closed the door, walked to the opposite side of the house, and crawled into bed. The concrete walls didn't **muffle** his **pitiful** cries. I lay there, trying to ignore them. I figured he would give up any minute and go to sleep.

The crying continued. Even after I wrapped my pillow around my head, I could still hear it. Poor Marley. Out there alone for the first time in his life. His mother was

pace (일정한 보조로) 걷다, (규칙적으로) 왔다갔다하다 perimeter 주변, 경계 audible 들리는 full-fledged 완전한, 완전히 성장한 torture 고문하다, 괴롭히다 pet 쓰다듬다, 어루만지다 yip 깽깽거리기 muffle (소리를) 죽이다 pitiful 동정심을 유발하는, 애처로운

missing in action, and so were all his brothers and sisters. There wasn't even a single dog *smell*.

I **hung on** for another half hour before getting up and going to him. As soon as he **spot**ted me, his face brightened and his tail began to beat the side of the box. It was as if he were saying, "Come on. Hop in. There's plenty of room."

Instead I lifted the box with him in it and carried it into my bedroom. I placed it on the floor against the side of the bed. I lay down on the very edge of the mattress, my arm **dangling** into the box. There, my hand resting on his side where I could feel his **rib cage** rise and fall with his every breath, we both **drifted off** to sleep.

hang on 기다리다 spot 발견하다 dangle 대롱대롱 매달리다 rib cage 갈비뼈, 흉곽 drift off (to sleep) 스르르 잠이 들다

Reading Comprehension

1. How much did the puppy grow after three weeks?

a. as big as an adult dog
b. twice as big as when Jenny and John first saw him
c. as big as a bag of puppy chow
d. five times as big as when Jenny and John first saw him

2. Jenny and John named their dog Marley after _____.

a. Bob Marley, the reggae singer
b. Bob Marley, the author's father
c. Bob Marley, their neighbor
d. Bob Marley, the president

3. Match the action to the tempo of Marley's tail wagging.

a. driving the car with both hands on the wheel (   )
b. one finger is touching Marley's head (   )
c. two fingers are touching Marley's head (   )
d. massaging Marley's head with all fingers (   )

1) Thump-thump-thump-thump-thump-thump!
2) Thumpthumpthumpthumpthumpthumpthumpthump!
3) Thump. Thump. Thump.
4) Thump-thumpa-thump-thump-thumpa-thump!

4. Where did Marley end up sleeping on his first night?

a. in the car garage   b. in the laundry   c. in the car   d. in the bedroom

Answers: **1.** b **2.** a **3.** a-3, b-1, c-4, d-2 **4.** d

3
Mr. Wiggles

For the next three days I threw myself into taking care of our new puppy. I lay on the floor with him and let him **scamper** all over me. I **wrestle**d with him. I used an old hand towel to play **tug-of-war** with him. Boy, was he strong! He followed me everywhere—and tried to gnaw on anything he could get his teeth around.

It took Marley just one day to discover the best thing about his new home—toilet paper. Five seconds after he disappeared into the bathroom, he came racing back out. As he **sprint**ed across the house with the end of the

---

scamper 종종걸음을 치다 wrestle 레슬링하다, 씨름하다 tug-of-war 줄다리기 sprint (단거리를) 질주하다, 달음질치다

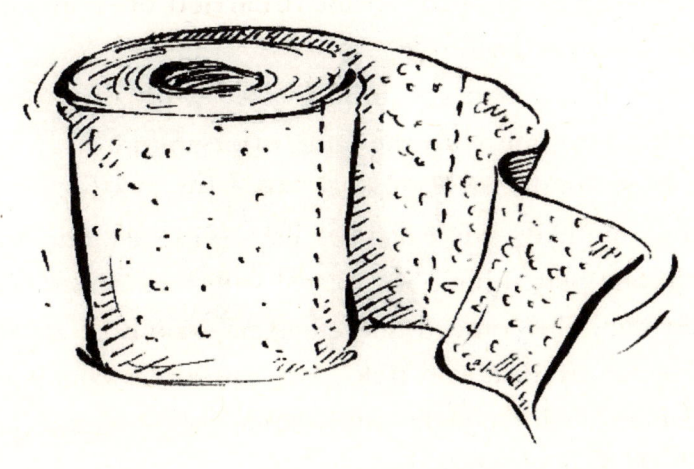

toilet-paper roll **clench**ed in his teeth, a paper ribbon unrolled behind him. The place looked like it had been decorated for Halloween.

Every half hour or so I would lead him into the backyard to **pee** or poop. When he had accidents in the house, I scolded him. When he peed outside, I placed my cheek against his and praised him in my sweetest voice. And when he pooped outside, I **carried on** as though we'd just won the lottery.

When Jenny returned from Disney World, she threw herself into him **with** the same **utter abandon**. It was amazing. As the days unfolded I saw in my young wife a gentle motherly side I had not known existed. She held him. She petted him. She played with him. She fussed over him. She combed through every **strand** of his fur in search of fleas and **tick**s. She rose every couple of hours through the night—night after night—to take him outside for bathroom breaks.

Mostly Jenny fed him.

Following the instructions on the bag, we gave Marley three large bowls of puppy chow a day. He **wolfed down** every **morsel** in a matter of seconds. Marley's

---

clench (이를) 악물다   pee 오줌을 누다   carry on 호들갑을 떨다   utter 전적인, 완전한   with abandon 저돌적으로, 앞뒤 가리지 않고   strand (끈이나 머리카락의) 가닥   tick 진드기   wolf down 게걸스럽게 먹어치우다   morsel 부스러기, 조각

appetite was huge, and his poop was huger still. The giant **mound**s that came out looked an awful lot like what he'd eaten earlier. Was he even digesting this stuff?

Apparently he was. Marley was growing at a furious pace. Each day he was a little longer, a little wider, a little taller, a little heavier. He was twenty-one pounds when I brought him home. Within weeks he was up to fifty. His cute little puppy head had rapidly morphed into something resembling the shape and **heft** of a **blacksmith**'s **anvil**.

Marley's paws were enormous. His **side**s already **ripple**d with muscle. His chest was almost as broad as a bulldozer. His little puppy tail was becoming as thick and powerful as an **otter**'s.

What a tail it was. Every last object in our house that was at knee level or below was knocked in all directions by Marley's wildly wagging weapon. He cleared coffee tables, scattered magazines, knocked framed photographs off shelves, and sent bottles and glasses flying. Gradually Jenny and I moved every item up to higher ground, safely above the **sweep** of his swinging **mallet**.

Marley didn't actually wag his tail. He wagged his whole

mound 무더기, heft 무게, 중량, blacksmith 대장장이, anvil 모루, side 몸의 측면, ripple 주름지다, 울룩불룩하다, otter 수달, sweep 휘두르기, 휩쓸기, mallet 망치

body, starting with the front shoulders and working backward. He was like the **canine** version of a **Slinky**. We swore there were no bones inside him—just one big, **elastic** muscle. Jenny began calling him Mr. Wiggles.

Marley wiggled most when he had something in his mouth. His reaction to any situation was the same. He would grab the nearest shoe or pillow or pencil and run with it. Really, any item would do. Some little voice in his head seemed to be whispering to him, "Go ahead! Pick it up! **Drool** all over it! Run!"

Some of the objects he grabbed were small enough to **conceal**, and this made him especially pleased. He seemed to think he was **getting away with** something. But when Marley had something to hide, he couldn't keep it to himself. He would explode into **hyperdrive**. His body would **quiver**, his head would **bob** from side to side, and his entire rear end would swing in a sort of **spastic** dance. We called it the Marley Mambo.

"All right, what have you got this time?" I'd say.

Marley would **waggle** his way around the room. His hips swayed and his head **flail**ed up and down like a **whinny**ing horse. He would be so overjoyed with his

canine 견공, 개   Slinky 장력스프링 장난감   elastic 탄력 있는, 신축성이 좋은   drool 침을 흘리다, 묻히다   conceal 숨기다, 감추다   get away with (나쁜 짓을 하고도) 빠져나가다, 벌을 피하다   hyperdrive 매우 흥분한 상태   quiver (몸을) 부르르 떨다   bob (고개를) 끄덕이다, 위아래로 흔들다   spastic (몸짓이) 촌스러운, 서투른   waggle (몸을) 이리저리 흔들다   flail 허우적대다, 이리저리 흔들리다   whinny (말이 기분 좋은 듯이) 히이힝 울다

forbidden prize he could not contain himself. When I would finally get him **corner**ed and **pry** open his jaws, I never came up empty-handed. There was always something he had **pluck**ed out of the trash or off the floor. As he got taller, he'd take it right off the dining room table. Paper towels, **wadded** Kleenex, grocery receipts, wine corks, paper clips, chess pieces, bottle caps. It was like a **junkyard** in there.

Most evenings after dinner Jenny and I **stroll**ed together with Marley along the **waterfront**. *Stroll* is probably the wrong word. Marley strolled like a runaway **locomotive** strolls. He **surge**d ahead, pulling on his leash with all his might, **choking** himself **hoarse** in the process. We yanked him back. He yanked us forward. We **tug**ged. He pulled. He **veer**ed left and right, **dart**ing to every mailbox and **shrub**, sniffing, panting, and peeing without fully stopping. He usually missed his target and got more pee on himself than the intended target. He circled behind us, wrapping the leash around our ankles. Then he **lurch**ed again, nearly **trip**ping us. When someone approached with another dog, Marley would **bolt** at them

---

forbidden 금지된 corner 구석으로 몰다 pry 비틀어 열다 pluck 뽑다, 꺼내다 wadded (동그랗게) 뭉친 junkyard 고물 창고 stroll 한가로이 거닐다, 어슬렁거리다 waterfront 물가 locomotive 기관차 surge 돌진하다, 돌격하다 choke 숨 막히게 하다 hoarse (목소리가) 쉰, 걸걸한 tug 세게 잡아당기다, 끌다 veer 방향을 바꾸다 dart 돌진하다 shrub 관목, 떨기나무 lurch 갑자기 움직이다, 비틀거리며 걷다 trip 걸려 넘어지게 하다, 발부리가 걸리게 하다 bolt (갑자기) 튀어나가다

joyously, **rear**ing up on his hind legs when he reached the end of the leash. He just wanted to make friends.

"He sure seems to love life," one dog owner commented. That just about said it all.

rear 뒷다리로 서다

Reading Comprehension

1. What did Marley eat?

a. food scraps and leftovers
b. puppy chow
c. toilet paper
d. anything he could get his teeth around

2. Match Marley's body parts with the right description.

a. head
b. chest
c. tail
d. jaws

1) broad as a bulldozer
2) like the shape of an anvil
3) like a junkyard
4) like a swinging mallet

3. The owners called Marley the following names, true or false?

a. Mr. Wiggles
b. Marley Mambo
c. Marley Mania
d. Life Lover

4. Which of these enjoyable activities could Marley not do?

a. to unroll toilet paper
b. to wag his tail
c. to hide something
d. to go for walks

Answers: **1.** b **2.** a-2, b-1, c-4, d-3 **3.** a:T, b:T, c:F, d:F **4.** c

4

Master and Beast

Marley was growing up *fast*. When he was small, his skin was so **droopy** that he looked like he was wearing an oversized yellow fur coat. By the time he was five months old, his body had **filled out** the wrinkles. His giant puppy paws no longer looked like canine clown feet. His needle-sharp baby teeth had turned into **fang**s that could destroy a **Frisbee** in a few quick **chomp**s. His high bark had deepened to a scary **boom**. When he stood on his hind legs, he could rest his paws on my shoulders and look me straight in the eye.

beast 짐승, 야수 droopy 축 늘어진 fill out 살이 찌다 fang 송곳니 Frisbee 프리스비, 원반 chomp 씹기 boom (쩌렁쩌렁) 울리는 소리

The first time the **vet** saw him, he let out a soft whistle and said, "You're going to have a big boy on your hands."

And we did.

We were not the only ones to notice. Our front door had a small **oblong** window at eye level. Marley **lived for** company. Whenever someone rang the bell, he would **streak** across the house. Then he'd go into a full **skid** as he approached the **foyer**. Sliding across the wood floors and **tossing up throw rug**s along the way, he didn't stop until he crashed into the door with a loud **thud**. At the door, he'd **hop up** on his hind legs and **yelp** wildly. His big head filled the tiny window as he stared straight into the face of whoever was on the other side. Terrified strangers ran from "the beast." They raced to the middle of the driveway and waited for someone to answer the door.

After breakfast one morning, Jenny and I decided to walk Marley down to the water for a swim. When we reached the little beach, I wagged a stick in front of Marley's face and took off his leash. He stared at the stick as if he were a starving man staring at a loaf of bread. His eyes never left the prize.

---

vet 수의사 oblong 사각형의 live for 사족을 못 쓰다 streak 질주하다 skid 미끄러지기, 미끄럼타기
foyer 로비, 현관 toss up 내던지다 throw rug 작은 깔개 thud 쿵, 털썩 hop up 뛰어오르다 yelp 왈왈 짖다

"Go get it!" I shouted, and **hurl**ed the stick as far out onto the water as I could. He galloped down the beach. As he entered the shallow water, **plume**s of spray **shot up** around him. This is what Labrador retrievers were born to do. It is in their **gene**s.

Labs are known for their desire to **fetch**. People **bred** these water dogs to help hunt birds. Once a bird was shot, the dogs would race to get it. Sometimes that meant **leap**ing into ice-cold water to get the dead animal and bring it back to the hunter. These loyal friends never expected a reward for their hard work.

Marley had **inherit**ed at least half of the instinct. He was a master at chasing his **prey**. He didn't quite get that he was supposed to return it. He might as well have said, "If you want the stick back that bad, YOU jump in the water for it."

Marley charged back up onto the beach with his prize in his teeth.

"Bring it here!" I yelled, slapping my hands together. "C'mon, boy, give it to me!" He **prance**d over, his whole body wagging with excitement, and shaking water and sand all over me.

---

hurl 내던지다, 내팽개치다 plume (연기, 먼지, 물 등의) 기둥 모양 shoot up 치솟다 gene 유전자 fetch 가져오다 breed 양육하다, 기르다 leap 뛰어오르다, 껑충 뛰다 inherit 유전되다, 물려받다 prey 먹잇감 prance (의기양양하게) 달리다, 걷다

To my surprise, Marley dropped the stick at my feet. *Wow*, I thought. *How's that for service?* But when I reached down to pick up the stick, Marley was ready. He dove in, grabbed it, and raced across the beach in crazy figure eights. He **swerve**d back, nearly **colliding** with me, **taunt**ing me to chase him. I made a few **lunge**s at him, but he was too fast and **agile**.

"You're supposed to be a Labrador retriever!" I shouted. "Not a Labrador **evader**!"

Maybe Marley had strength, but I had brains. I grabbed a second stick and made a big deal about it. I held it over my head and tossed it from hand to hand. I swung it from side to side. He **crept** closer until he was just inches in front of me. I rubbed the stick across his **snout** and watched as he went **cross-eyed** trying to keep it in his sights.

The little **cog**s turned in his head. He tried to figure out how he could grab the new stick without giving up the old one. His upper lip quivered.

"I wonder if I could make a quick two-for-one grab," he seemed to be asking himself. Soon I had my free hand firmly around the end of the stick in his mouth. I tugged

---

swerve 갑자기 방향을 바꾸다, 급선회하다 collide 충돌하다 taunt 도발하다, 놀리다 lunge 돌진 agile 민첩한 evader 피하는 사람 creep 기다 snout (돌출된) 코, 주둥이 cross-eyed 사팔눈을 뜨는 cog 톱니바퀴

and he tugged back, **growl**ing.

I pressed the second stick against his **nostril**s. "You know you want it," I whispered. And did he ever. The temptation was too much to bear. I could feel his grip loosening. And then he made his move. He opened his jaws to try to grab the second stick without losing the first. **In a heartbeat**, I **whip**ped both sticks high above my head. He leaped in the air, barking and spinning, obviously **at a loss** to how such a carefully laid battle plan could have gone so wrong.

"This is why I am the master and you are the beast," I told him.

In response, Marley shook water and sand in my face.

I threw one of the sticks out into the water and he raced after it, yelping madly as he went. When he returned he was a new, wiser opponent. This time he was **cautious** and refused to come anywhere near me. He stood about ten yards away, stick in mouth, eyeing the new object of his desire. It just happened to be the old object of his desire, his first stick. Now it was **perch**ed high above my head. I could see the cogs moving again. He was thinking, "This time I'll just wait right here until

---

growl 으르렁거리다 nostril 콧구멍 in a heartbeat 곧장, 즉시 whip 휘두르다, 휙 움직이다 at a loss 어찌할 바를 모르는 cautious 신중한, 조심하는 perch 놓다, 앉히다

he throws it, then he'll have no sticks and I'll have both sticks."

"You think I'm really dumb, don't you, dog?" I said. I **heave**d back and hurled the stick with all my might. Marley roared into the water with his stick still locked in his teeth. The only thing was, I hadn't let go of mine. Do you think Marley figured that out? He swam halfway across the water before catching on that the stick was still in my hand.

"You're cruel!" Jenny yelled down from her bench, laughing.

When Marley finally got back **onshore**, he **plopped down** in the sand. Although he was exhausted, he was not about to give up his stick. I showed him mine and reminded him how much better it was than his.

"Drop it!" I ordered. I **cock**ed my arm back as if to throw. The dumb dog bolted back to his feet and began heading for the water again. "Drop it!" I repeated when he returned. It took several tries, but finally he did just that. And the instant his stick hit the sand, I **launch**ed mine into the air for him. We did it over and over, and each time he seemed to understand a little more clearly.

---

heave 올리다, 들다　onshore 물으로, 육지 쪽으로　plop down (툭 소리를 내며) 주저앉다　cock (던지거나 치기 위해) 뒤로 젖히다　launch 내던지다

Slowly the lesson was **sinking into** that thick **skull** of his. If he returned his stick to me, I would throw a new one for him.

"You've got to give to get," I told him. He leaped up and gave me a **sloppy**, sandy kiss. I guess that meant he'd learned his lesson.

As Jenny and I walked home, the **tuckered** Marley for once did not **strain** against his leash. "You know," I said to Jenny, "I really think he's starting to get it."

Jenny looked down at him, **plod**ding along beside us. He was soaking wet and coated in sand, **spittle foam**ing on his lips. He clenched his prize stick in his jaws.

"I wouldn't be so sure of that," she said.

---

sink into 새겨지다, 각인되다 skull 두개골, 머리 sloppy 질퍽한, 축축한 tuckered 지친, 녹초가 된
strain 팽팽하게 잡아당기다 plod 터벅터벅 걷다 spittle 침 foam 거품을 형성하다

Reading Comprehension

1. Identify the changes that occurred in Marley as he grew. Choose the right word.

In five months, Marley grew (quickly/slowly).
His fur used to be (droopy/fitted).
His baby (paws/teeth) grew into fangs, and his bark was now (higher/deeper).

2. What did the vet say to the Grogans?

a. "Wow, your dog is smelly."
b. "Get that crazy dog away from me!"
c. "You're going to have a big boy on your hands."
d. "You should put your dog on a diet."

3. What did John try to teach Marley at the beach?

a. to fetch the stick and then run away
b. to fetch the stick and return it to him to get another stick thrown
c. to swim after an imaginary stick and fetch it
d. to fetch the stick and get a sloppy kiss

4. What does "tuckered" mean?

a. to eat a lot
b. to tuck away your tongue
c. to be tired or exhausted
d. to be obedient

 1. quickly, droopy, teeth, deeper **2.** c **3.** b **4.** c

5

A Battle of Wills

When Marley was not quite six months old, we signed him up for **obedience** classes. He definitely needed it. Despite his stick-fetching breakthrough on the beach that day, he was proving himself a challenging student—**dense**, wild, and constantly **distracted**. We were beginning to figure out that he was not like other dogs. We needed professional help.

Our **veterinarian** told us about a local dog-training club that offered basic obedience classes. When we went to register Marley, we met the woman who would be

---

obedience 복종, 순종 dense 우둔한 distracted 산만한 veterinarian 수의사

teaching our class. She was a **stern**, no-nonsense dog trainer who believed that there are no bad dogs, only weak-willed and hapless owners.

As Jenny, Marley, and I arrived for the first lesson, Marley spotted the other dogs gathering with their owners across the **tarmac**.

"A party!" he barked. He leaped over us and out of the car. He was off in a tear, his leash dragging behind him. He darted from one dog to the next, sniffing private parts, **dribbl**ing pee, and **fling**ing huge **wad**s of spit through the air. Sniff sniff. Dribble dribble. Fling fling. For Marley it was a festival of smells. He stayed just ahead of me as I raced after him. Each time I was nearly upon him, he would **scoot** a few feet farther away.

I finally got close. Taking a giant leap, I landed hard with both feet on the leash. He stopped with a sudden **jerk**. For a second, I was convinced I'd broken his neck. He jerked backward, **land**ed on his back, flipped around, and gazed up at me with the **serene** expression of a kid who has just eaten every last piece of candy in the candy store.

Meanwhile, the instructor was staring at us as if I had

---

stern 엄격한 tarmac (아스팔트 포장재) 타맥 dribble (액체를) 똑똑 흘리다 fling 내던지다, 내팽개치다 wad 뭉치, 덩어리 scoot 서둘러 가다 jerk (움찔하는) 급격한 동작/행동 land 착지하다 serene 침착한, 평온한

thrown off my clothes and danced naked right there on the **blacktop**. She was not amused.

"Take your place, please," she said **curtly**. Jenny and I tugged Marley into position. "You are going to have to decide which of you is going to be the trainer," she added.

The instructor didn't understand that we both wanted to participate so each of us could work with him at home. I decided to explain.

"But we—" I began.

"A dog can only answer to one master," she said, cutting me off.

"But—" I said. This time her **glare silence**d me. I **slunk** to the sidelines with my tail between my legs, leaving Master Jenny **in command**.

This was probably a mistake. Marley was already way stronger than Jenny and knew it. The instructor began her introduction on the importance of establishing **dominance** over our pets. That's when Marley spotted the standard poodle on the opposite side of the class. He **lunge**d off, with Jenny **in tow**.

All the other dogs sat ten feet apart, beside their

---

blacktop 아스팔트 curtly 딱 잘라서, 무뚝뚝하게 glare 노려보는 눈초리 silence 침묵시키다 slink 살금살금 걷다/움직이다 in command 주도권(명령권)을 쥔 dominance 지배, 우세 lunge 갑자기 튀어나가(오)다, 돌진하다 in tow 질질 끌려가는

masters. They waited for instructions. Jenny was fighting to plant her feet and bring Marley to a **halt**.

"Forward ho!" Marley seemed to be telling her. He **lumber**ed on and tugged her across the parking lot in pursuit of hot poodle butt-sniffing action. Jenny looked like a water-skier being towed behind a powerboat. Everyone stared. Some **snicker**ed. I covered my eyes.

Marley crashed into the poodle. Everyone waited as he sniffed every inch of her. I imagined it was his way of saying, "Nice to meet you!" Jenny tugged with all of her might, but Marley ignored her. "I'm not done yet," he seemed to be saying. Finally he finished saying his hellos, and Jenny was able to drag him back into place.

"That, class, is an example of a dog that has been allowed to think he is the **alpha male** of his pack," the instructor announced calmly. "Right now, he's in charge." Marley agreed by attacking his tail, spinning wildly as his jaws snapped at thin air. In the process he wrapped the leash around Jenny's ankles until she was fully **immobilize**d. I **wince**d and was thankful that it wasn't me out there.

The instructor showed the class how to command dogs

halt 정지, 멈춤   lumber 터덜터덜 걷다   snicker (킥킥) 비웃다   alpha male 우두머리 수컷/남성
immobilize 꼼짝 못하게 하다   wince 얼굴을 찡그리다, 쓴웃음을 짓다

to sit.

"Sit!" Jenny ordered. Marley jumped on her and put his paws on her shoulders. She pressed his butt to the ground. He **rolled over** for a **belly** rub. She tried to tug him into place. He grabbed the leash in his teeth, shaking his head from side to side as if he were wrestling a **python**.

It was too painful to watch. At one point, I opened my eyes to see Jenny lying on the **pavement facedown**. Marley stood over her, panting happily. She later told me she was trying to show him the **down command**.

Class ended, and Jenny and Marley rejoined me. So did the teacher.

"You really need to get control over that animal," she said with a **sneer**.

"Well, thank you for that valuable advice. Actually, we signed up just to make the rest of the class laugh." At least, that's what I wanted to say. Actually, neither of us breathed a word. We just retreated to the car in humiliation and drove home in silence. The only sound was Marley's loud, excited panting.

Finally I broke the silence. "He sure loves school!" I said.

---

roll over 구르다   belly 배, 복부   python 이무기, 비단뱀   pavement 포장도로   facedown 얼굴을 숙이고
down command '엎드려' 명령   sneer 비웃음, 비웃는 표정

The next week Marley and I were back, but this time without Jenny. When I suggested to her that I was probably the closest thing to an alpha dog we were going to find in our home, she gladly **relinquish**ed her brief title as master and commander. Before leaving the house, I flipped Marley over on his back, **towered over** him, and growled in my most **intimidating** voice, "I'm the boss! You're not the boss! I'm the boss! Got it, Alpha Dog?" He **thump**ed his tail on the floor and tried to gnaw on my wrists.

The night's lesson was walking on heel. I was eager to master it. I was tired of fighting Marley every step of every walk. Jenny was, too. Once he took off after a cat and yanked her off her feet, leaving her with bloody knees. It was time he learned to **trot** by our sides.

I wrestled him to our spot on the tarmac, pulling him back from every dog we passed along the way.

"Class, on the count of three," the instructor called out. "One . . . two . . . three."

"Marley, **heel**!" I commanded. As soon as I took my first step, he shot off like a fighter jet from an **aircraft carrier**. I yanked back hard on the leash. He coughed

---

relinquish (권리 따위를) 포기하다　tower over (~를) 굽어보다　intimidate 협박하다, 겁주다　thump (쿵/탁 소리가 나게) 때리다　trot 종종걸음을 걷다　heel 바짝 붙어 걷다, 따라와!　aircraft carrier 항공모함

and gasped as the collar tightened around his airway. He sprang back for an instant, then lunged forward again. I yanked back. He gasped again. We continued like this the entire length of the parking lot. He was coughing and panting. I was **grunt**ing and sweating.

"**Rein** that dog **in**!" the instructor yelled. I tried with all my might, but the lesson wasn't sinking in. I thought that Marley might just **strangle** himself before he figured it out. Meanwhile, the other dogs were prancing along at their owners' sides.

The instructor had the class line up and try again. Once again, Marley lurched like a maniac across the blacktop. With his eyes **bulging**, he strangled himself as he went.

"Here," the instructor said impatiently. "Let me show you." I handed the leash to her. She tugged Marley around into position. She pulled up on the **collar** as she ordered him to sit. Sure enough, he sat, eagerly looking up at her.

With a yank of the leash, the instructor **set off** with him. Almost instantly he barreled ahead as if he were pulling the lead sled in a dogsled race. She corrected

grunt 구시렁거리다, 끙끙대다   rein in 통제하다, 제지하다   strangle ~의 목을 조르다   bulge 튀어나오다, 불거지다   collar (개나 고양이의) 목걸이   set off 출발하다

hard, pulling him off balance. He stumbled, **wheeze**d, then lunged forward again. It looked like he was going to pull her arm out of its **socket**. I should have been embarrassed. But I felt an odd sort of satisfaction. She wasn't having any more success than I was. My classmates snickered, and I **beam**ed with **perverse** pride. I wanted to yell, "See, my dog is awful for everyone, not just me!"

I had to admit, the scene was pretty **hilarious**. The two of them reached the end of the parking lot. Then they turned and lurched back toward us.

The instructor **scowl**ed with rage. Marley was joyous beyond words. She yanked furiously at the leash. **Slobber**ing with excitement, Marley yanked back harder still. I could tell what he was thinking. "All right! Tug-of-war."

When Marley saw me, he **hit the gas**. Filled with near-supernatural speed, he **made a dash** for me. The instructor broke into a sprint to keep from being pulled off her feet. Marley didn't stop until he **slam**med into me with his usual **exuberance**.

The instructor shot me a look that told me I was in trouble. Marley had made a **mockery** of her class. He

---

wheeze 씨근거리다 socket 푹 들어간 곳, 구멍 beam 활짝 웃다 perverse (태도나 성향이) 비뚤어진, 비딱한 hilarious 대단히 신나는, 유쾌한 scowl 인상을 쓰다, 얼굴을 찌푸리다 slobber 침을 흘리다 hit the gas 속도를 높이다 make a dash 돌진하다 slam 충돌하다 exuberance 활력이 넘치는 행동 mockery 조롱, 놀림감

had **publicly** humiliated her.

The instructor handed the leash back to me. "Okay, class, on the count of three . . . ," she said, pretending the whole thing hadn't even happened.

When the lesson was over, she asked if I could stay after for a minute. "I think your dog is still a little young for structured obedience training," she explained.

"He's a **handful**, isn't he?" I said. Now that we had shared the same **humiliating** experience, I felt as though we were friends.

"He's simply not ready for this," she said. "He has some growing up to do."

It was beginning to **dawn** on me what she was getting at. "Are you trying to tell me—"

"He's a **distraction** to the other dogs."

"—that you're—"

"He's just too **excitable**."

"—kicking us out of class?"

"You can always bring him back in another six or eight months."

"So you're kicking us out?"

"I'll happily give you a full refund."

publicly 공개적으로　handful 말을 잘 듣지 않거나 다루기 힘든 사람/것　humiliate 망신을 주다　dawn 감이 잡히다, 이해가 가다　distraction 주의집중을 방해하는 것　excitable 쉽게 흥분하는

"You're kicking us out."

"Yes," she finally said. "I'm kicking you out."

Marley lifted his leg and let loose a **raging** stream of pee, nearly hitting his beloved instructor's foot.

Sometimes a man needs to get angry to get serious. The instructor had made me angry. I owned a beautiful, **purebred** Labrador retriever, a proud member of the breed famous for its ability to guide the blind, rescue disaster victims, assist hunters, and pluck fish from big ocean **swell**s, all with calm intelligence. How dare she **write** him **off** after just two lessons? Okay, he was a bit on the **spirited** side, but his intentions were all good.

I was going to prove to that **insufferable** stuffed shirt that she could kick us out, but Marley was no **quitter**. He would show her!

First thing the next morning, Marley was out in the backyard with me. "Nobody kicks the Grogan boys out of obedience school," I told him. "**Untrainable**? We'll see who's untrainable. Right?" He bounced up and down. "Can we do it, Marley?" He wiggled. "I can't hear you! Can we do it?" He yelped. "That's better. Now let's get to work."

---

raging 맹렬한, (강물이) 세차게 몰아치는 purebred 순종의 swell 파도의 움직임 write off 쓸모 없다고 단정하다 spirited 활달한 insufferable 밉상인, 비위에 거슬리는 quitter 쉽게 포기하는 자 untrainable 길들일 수 없는, 훈련이 불가능한

We started with the sit command, which I had been practicing with him since he was a small puppy. He was already quite good at it. I towered over him and gave him my best alpha-dog scowl.

"Sit," I said in a firm but calm voice. He sat. "Good boy!" I praised.

We repeated the exercise several times. Next we moved to the down command, another one I had been practicing with him. He stared intently into my eyes, neck straining forward, **anticipating** my **directive**.

I slowly raised my hand in the air and held it there as he waited for the word. With a sharp downward motion, I snapped my fingers, pointed at the ground and said, "Down!" Marley collapsed in a heap, hitting the ground with a thud. He went down **with gusto**—as if a **mortar shell** just exploded behind him.

Jenny, sitting on the porch with her coffee, noticed it, too. "**Incoming**!" she yelled out.

After several rounds of hit-the-deck, I moved up to the next challenge—come on command. This was a tough one for Marley. The coming part was not the problem; it was waiting in place until we called him. He was so

---

anticipate 기대하다 directive 명령 with gusto 기꺼이, 즐겁게 mortar shell 박격포 포탄 incoming 다가오는, 다가오기

anxious to be **plaster**ed against us that he could not sit still while we walked away from him.

"Sit," I commanded. He faced me, and I fixed my eyes on his. As we stared at each other, I raised my palm, holding it out in front of me like a crossing guard. "Stay," I said, and took a step backward. He froze, staring anxiously, waiting for the slightest sign he could join me. On my fourth step backward, he could take it no longer and broke free, racing up and **tumbling** against me. I scolded him and tried it again. And again and again.

Each time he allowed me to get a little farther away before charging. Eventually I stood fifty feet across the yard, with my palm out toward him. I stood and waited. He sat, locked in position, his entire body quaking with anticipation. I could see the nervous energy building in him. He was like a volcano ready to blow. But he stayed. I counted to ten. He did not **budge**. His eyes froze on me. His muscles bulged. Okay, enough torture.

I dropped my hand and yelled, "Marley, come!"

As he **catapult**ed forward, I squatted down and clapped my hands to encourage him. I thought he might go racing **willy-nilly** across the yard, but he **made a**

---

plaster 찰싹 달라붙다   tumble 넘어지다, 구르다   budge 움직이다   catapult 나는 듯이 돌진하다   willy-nilly 마구잡이로, 닥치는 대로   make a beeline for ~를 향해 곧장 가다(오다)

beeline straight **for** me. *Perfect!* I thought.

"C'mon, boy! C'mon!" I coached. He was barreling right at me. "Slow it down, boy," I said. He just kept coming. "Slow down!" He had this **vacant**, crazed look on his face. It was a one-dog stampede. I had time for one final command. "STOP!!!" I screamed.

***Blam*!** He **plow**ed into me without **breaking stride**. I **pitch**ed backward, slamming hard to the ground. When I opened my eyes a few seconds later, he was **straddling** me with all four paws, lying on my chest and desperately licking my face.

"How did I do, boss?" my proud puppy seemed to be asking.

Technically speaking, he had followed orders exactly. After all, I had failed to mention anything about stopping once he got to me.

"Mission accomplished," I said with a **groan**.

Jenny peered out the kitchen window. "I'm off to work." she shouted. "When you two are done **making out**, don't forget to close the windows. It's supposed to rain this afternoon." I gave **Linebacker** Dog a snack and then showered and headed off myself to my job as a

---

vacant 멍한, 얼빠진 blam 쿵/퍽 하는 소리 plow 충돌하다, 들이받다 break (one's) stride 걸음의 속도를 줄이다, ~한 기세를 꺾다 pitch 쾅당 넘어지다 straddle 다리를 벌리고 서다(앉다) groan 신음 make out 키스하고 만지며 애정표현 하다 linebacker (미식축구에서) 수비수

newspaper reporter.

When I arrived home that night, Jenny was waiting for me at the front door. I could tell she was upset.

"Go look in the garage," she said.

I opened the door into the garage, and the first thing I spotted was Marley, lying on his carpet, looking sad.

My mind took a photo of the scene. Marley's snout and front paws were not right. They were dark brown, not their usual light yellow. It took me a few seconds to figure out that they were covered in dried blood. Then my focus zoomed out and I **sucked in my breath**. We had thought the garage was indestructible, but Marley had destroyed it. **Throw rug**s were **shred**ded. Paint was **clawed off** the concrete walls. The ironing board was **tipped over**, its fabric cover hanging in ribbons.

Worst of all, the doorway in which I stood looked like it had been attacked with a **chipper-shredder**. Bits of wood were sprayed in a ten-foot semicircle around the door, which had a hole halfway through to the other side. The bottom three feet of the **doorjamb** was missing entirely and nowhere to be found. Blood **streak**ed the

suck in one's breath 숨이 턱 막히다　throw rug 작은 깔개　shred 갈기갈기 찢다　claw A off B 발톱으로 긁어 A를 B에서 벗겨 내다　tip over 넘어지다, 뒤집히다　chipper-shredder 파쇄기　doorjamb 문설주　streak 흘러내리다

walls from where Marley had shredded his paws and **muzzle**.

"I don't believe it," I said, more amazed than angry.

"When I came home for lunch, everything was fine," Jenny said from behind me. "But I could tell it was getting ready to rain." After she was back at work, an **intense** storm had moved through, bringing with it sheets of rain and **dazzling** flashes of lightning. The thunder was so powerful you could actually feel it thump against your chest.

While the storm **rage**d, Marley had desperately tried to escape. The storm had sent him into a complete, **panic-stricken frenzy**. Alone and terrified as the storm came, Marley had decided his best chance at survival was to begin digging his way into the house. When Jenny arrived home a couple hours later, Marley stood in the middle of the mess he had made.

But it didn't take long for Marley to forget the whole incident. Back to his old self, he grabbed a chew toy and bounced around us, looking for a little tug-of-war action. I held him still while Jenny **sponge**d the blood off his fur. Then he watched us, tail wagging, as we cleaned up

---

muzzle 주둥이 intense 극심한 dazzling 눈부신, 휘황찬란한 rage 맹위를 떨치다 panic-stricken 공황 상태에 빠진, 공포심에 사로잡혀 어찌할 바를 모르는 frenzy 광란, 발작 sponge 스펀지로 닦다

his handiwork.

"You don't have to look so happy about it." I scowled and brought him inside for the night.

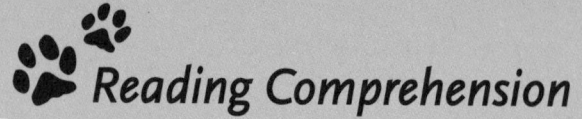
Reading Comprehension

1. How did Marley greet other dogs?

a. He said hello politely.
b. He sniffed them all over.
c. He barked at them.
d. He bit them.

2. Which of the following is not the reason why Marley was kicked out of obedience school?

a. He was uncontrollable.
b. He embarrassed the instructor.
c. He was too young to learn.
d. He bit the other dogs.

3. Match the commands with the actions.

a. Sit!   1) Marley comes charging forward.
b. Down!   2) Marley puts his rear on the ground.
c. Come!   3) Marley collapses his whole body to the ground.
d. Stay!   4) Marley remains still.

4. Which best describes how Marley felt about storms?

a. nervous and excited   b. happy and joyful
c. scared and terrified   d. angry and upset

Answers: **1.** b **2.** d **3.** a-2, b-3, c-1, d-4 **4.** c

6

The Great Escape

One thing was clear. Jenny and I loved our dog, but having a bunch of little Marleys running around in the world was not a good idea. It was time to make sure Marley couldn't make any puppies. Jenny and I decided to have him **fix**ed so he would never be a father.

As we got ready to take Marley to the vet, he bounced happily off the walls. "Yippee!" his excited movements told us. He could tell he was going for a car ride, and he didn't care where.

For Marley, any trip was a good trip. It didn't matter

fix (동물을) 거세하다

where we were going or for how long. Take out the trash? "No problem!" Walk to the corner for a **gallon** of milk? "**Count** me **in**!"

When I whistled, Marley bounded out the door and into the car. He was **revved up** and ready to go. Jenny drove and I sat in the passenger seat. Marley balanced his front paws on the center console—just like he always did. His nose touched the rearview mirror. Every time Jenny pressed the brakes, he went crashing into the **windshield**. Marley didn't care. He was **riding shotgun** with his two best friends.

"Life doesn't get any better than this," his puppy joy announced.

I rolled down my window a bit and Marley leaned against me, trying to catch a **whiff** of the outdoor smells. Soon he squirmed his way fully onto my lap. He pressed his nose so firmly into the narrow crack of the window that he snorted each time he tried to **inhale**.

"Do you want a little more fresh air, buddy?" I asked. I opened up the window wide enough for him to stick his snout out. He was enjoying the sensation so much, I opened it farther. Soon his entire head was out the

gallon (용량의 단위) 갤론, 약 3.78리터　count in 끼워주다, 포함하다　rev up 사기를/흥을 북돋다
windshield 자동차 앞 유리창　ride shotgun (차의) 조수석에 타다　whiff 휙 일어나는 냄새/바람/연기
inhale 숨을 들이마시다

window. His tongue hung out and his ears **flap**ped behind him in the wind. Was he happy!

As we drove down the highway, Jenny and I talked. Pretty soon I noticed that Marley had hooked both of his front paws over the edge of the half-open window. And now his neck and upper shoulders were hanging out of the car, too. He just needed a pair of goggles and a silk scarf to look like one of those World War I flying aces.

"John, he's making me nervous," Jenny said.

"He's fine," I answered. "He just wants a little fresh—"

At that instant he slid his front legs out the window until his **armpit**s were resting on the edge of the glass.

"John, grab him! Grab him!" Jenny yelled.

Before I could do anything, Marley was scrambling out the window of our moving car. His butt was up in the air, and his hind legs were **claw**ing for something to hold on to. He was making his break!

As his body **slither**ed past me, I lunged for him and managed to grab the end of his tail with my left hand. Jenny was braking hard even though there was traffic all around us. Marley's entire body dangled outside the moving car, hanging upside down by his tail. My body

---

flap 펄럭이다, 휘날리다   armpit 겨드랑이   claw (발톱이 달린 발로) 버둥대다, 발길질을 하다   slither 주르르 미끄러지다

was twisted around, and I couldn't get my other hand on him. Marley was **frantically** trotting along with his front paws on the pavement.

Jenny stopped the car in the left-hand lane. Cars lined up behind us. Their **horn**s **blare**d.

"Now what?" I yelled. I was **stuck**. I couldn't pull him back in the window. I couldn't open the door. I couldn't get my other arm out. And I didn't **dare let** go of him—I was convinced he'd **dash** in the path of one of the angry drivers **swerving** around us. With my face **scrunch**ed against the glass, I held on for dear life.

Jenny put on the car's **flasher**s and ran around to my side. She grabbed Marley and held him by the collar until I could get out and help her wrestle him back into the car.

All the action had taken place directly in front of a gas station. As Jenny got the car moving again, I looked over to see that all the mechanics had come out to take in the show. I thought they were going to pee in their pants, they were laughing so hard.

"Thanks, guys!" I called out. "Glad we could brighten your morning."

---

frantically 미친 듯이, 정신 없이 horn 경적 blare 크게 울리다, 소음을 내다 stuck 꼼짝하지 못하는, 이러지도 저러지도 못하는 dare (to) do 감히 ~하다 dash 돌진하다, 질주하다 swerve 방향을 바꾸어 피하다 scrunch 짓이기다, 뭉개다 flasher 비상등, 깜빡이등

Reading Comprehension

1. What was Marley most excited about?

a. seeing the vet
b. being fixed
c. never having puppies
d. going for a car ride

2. Place the following scenes in the correct order.

a. Marley's head is sticking out the window with his tongue hanging out and his ears flapping.
b. Marley is trotting along on his front paws hanging outside the car while it's still moving.
c. Marley is sitting on John's lap with his nose sniffing the air through a slightly open window.
d. Marley's front legs are out of the car and his armpits are resting on the edge of the glass.

3. What did John do to try to help Marley?

a. He pulled him back in through the window.
b. He opened the door.
c. He let go of Marley, so he could run away.
d. He just held on and didn't let go.

4. What did the mechanics think of Marley's antics?

a. angry that he had held up traffic
b. scornful that he was such a bad dog
c. humored because it had looked funny
d. scared because Marley was a big dog trying to escape

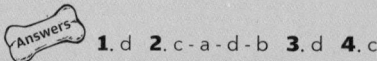

Answers: **1.** d **2.** c - a - d - b **3.** d **4.** c

7

The Things He Ate

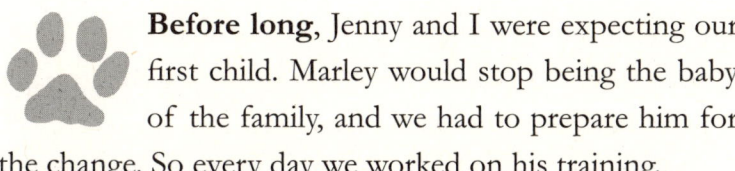**Before long**, Jenny and I were expecting our first child. Marley would stop being the baby of the family, and we had to prepare him for the change. So every day we worked on his training.

Now I was able to entertain our friends by yelling, "Incoming!" and watching Marley crash to the floor, all four **limb**s **splay**ed.

He always came **on command**—unless something caught his attention, such as another dog, squirrel, butterfly, mailman, or floating weed seed. He always sat—unless he felt like standing. He always heeled—unless

before long 머지않아　limb 팔다리　splay 널브러지다, 쭉 뻗다　on command 명령을 받고, 명령에 따라

there was something so tempting it was worth strangling himself over, such as another dog, squirrel, butterfly . . . Well, you get the idea.

Marley's training was coming along. But that didn't mean he was **mellow**ing into a calm, well-behaved dog. If I towered over him and barked **stern** orders, he would obey. Sometimes he'd even do it eagerly. But Marley was still Marley. And Marley was **incorrigible**.

A giant mango tree grew in our Florida backyard, and mangoes **rained down** to the ground. Marley could never eat enough. Each weighed a pound or more. They were so sweet they could make your teeth ache. Marley would stretch out in the grass, **anchor** a ripe mango between his front paws, and remove every bit of **flesh** from the skin. It was as if he were performing surgery. He would hold the large **pit**s in his mouth like **lozenge**s. When he finally spit them out, they looked like they had been cleaned in an acid bath. There was not **a speck of** fruit left on them. Some days he would be out there for hours, frantically **gobbling** down mango after mango.

When you eat lots of fruit, you get lots of poop. Soon

---

mellow 성숙하다, 점잖아지다　stern 단호한, 엄격한　incorrigible 제멋대로 구는, 막무가내인　rain down 비가 오듯 쏟아지다　anchor 고정시키다　flesh 과육　pit 과일의 씨　lozenge 마름모꼴의 사탕　a speck of 소량의, 약간의　gobble (down/up) 게걸스럽게 먹다

our backyard was **litter**ed with large piles of **festively colored** dog droppings. The one advantage to this was that it was nearly impossible to accidentally step in a heap of his poop, which **glow**ed like orange **traffic cone**s.

Mangoes weren't the only item coming out in the poop piles. Marley also ate other things, and these, too, came out the other end. I saw the evidence each morning as I **shoveled up** his piles. Here a toy plastic soldier, there a rubber band. In one load a **mangle**d soda-bottle top. In another the gnawed cap to a ballpoint pen.

"So that's where my comb went!" I **exclaim**ed one morning.

Marley ate bath towels, sponges, socks, and used Kleenex. Handi Wipes were one of his favorites. When they came out, they looked like little blue flags marking each **fluorescent** mango mountain.

Not everything went down easily, and Marley vomited easily and often.

Gaaaaack! When we heard the noise, we knew Marley had puked. By the time we rushed into the room, there would be another household item, sitting in a **puddle** of half-digested mangoes and dog chow. Marley never puked

litter 어지르다 festively colored 총천연색의 glow 뭉근한 빛을 내다 traffic cone 원뿔형의 도로 표지 shovel up (삽으로) 뜨다, 푸다 mangle 토막 내다, 짓뭉개다 exclaim 외치다, 고함을 지르다 fluorescent 형광색의 puddle 웅덩이

on the hardwood floors or even the kitchen **linoleum** if he could help it. He always aimed for the fancy rug.

Jenny and I decided that it would be nice to have a dog we could trust to be alone in the house. We were tired of locking him in the garage every time we stepped out. And as Jenny said, "What's the point of having a dog if he can't greet you at the door when you get home?"
　We began leaving him briefly while we ran to the store or **dropped by** a neighbor's house. When he behaved himself, he would push his black nose through the miniblinds and stare out the living room window, waiting for us. When he hadn't behaved, he hid.
　Once we were gone for less than an hour. Marley was under the bed. (And at his size, he really had to work to get under there.) He looked like he'd just murdered the mailman. The house seemed fine, but we knew he was hiding some dark secret. Guilt **radiated off** him like heat off the sun. We walked from room to room, trying to figure out what he had done wrong. Then I noticed that the **foam cover** to one of the stereo speakers was missing. We looked everywhere for it. It was gone

linoleum (바닥재의 일종) 리놀륨　drop by 들르다　radiate off (~에게서) 발산되다, 풍기다　foam cover 스펀지 커버

without a trace. Marley nearly got away with it. But I found evidence of his guilt when I went on poop patrol the next morning. Pieces of the speaker cover surfaced for days.

During our next **outing**, Marley removed the **woofer cone** from the same speaker. The speaker wasn't knocked over. It wasn't out of place at all. The part was simply gone, as if someone had sliced it with a **razor blade**. Eventually he got around to doing the same to the other speaker.

Another time, he turned our four-legged **footstool** into a three-legged footstool. Not a single **splinter** was left.

We swore it could never snow in South Florida, but one day we opened the front door to find a **blizzard** in the living room. The air was filled with soft white **fluff** floating down. We spotted Marley in front of the fireplace, half buried in a **snowdrift**, violently shaking a large feather pillow from side to side as though he had just captured an **ostrich**.

For the most part we accepted the damage. After all, in every dog owner's life a few precious items get chewed, broken, or totally destroyed. One time, though, I was

---

outing 외출 woofer cone 저음 확성기 razor blade 면도날 footstool (발을 올려놓고 쉬는) 발 받침대 splinter 부서진 조각 blizzard 눈보라 fluff 솜털, 보풀 snowdrift (바람에 의해 쌓인) 눈 더미 ostrich 타조

desperate. I was ready to do whatever it took to get what was mine—or Jenny's, actually.

For her birthday I had bought Jenny an eighteen-karat gold necklace, a delicate chain with a tiny **clasp**. She immediately put it on.

A few hours later she pressed her hand to her throat. "My necklace!" she screamed. "It's gone."

"Don't panic," I told her. "We haven't left the house. It's got to be right here somewhere." We began **scour**ing the house, room by room. As we searched, I gradually became aware that Marley was more **rambunctious** than usual. I **straightened up** and looked at him. He was squirming like a **centipede**. When he noticed I had him in my sights, he began **evasive** action. *Oh, no,* I thought, the Marley Mambo. It could mean only one thing.

"What's that," Jenny asked, panic rising in her voice, "hanging out of his mouth?"

It was thin and delicate. And gold. "Oh, shoot!" I said.

"Don't make any sudden moves," she ordered, her voice dropping to a whisper. We both froze.

"Okay, boy, it's all right," I **coax**ed like a **hostage** negotiator on a SWAT team. "We're not mad at you.

---

clasp 걸쇠 scour 샅샅이 뒤지다, 수색하다 rambunctious 날뛰는 straighten up 몸을 똑바로 일으키다
centipede 지네 evasive 꽁무니를 빼는, 슬금슬금 피하는 coax 꼬시다, 구슬리다 hostage 인질

Come on now. We just want the necklace back." **Instinctively** Jenny and I began to circle him from opposite directions, moving as slowly as **glacier**s. It was as if he were **wire**d with **high explosive**s and one false move could **set** him **off**.

"Easy, Marley," Jenny said in her calmest voice. "Easy now. Drop the necklace and no one gets hurt."

Marley eyed us suspiciously, his head darting back and forth between us. We had him cornered, but he knew he had something we wanted. I could see him weighing his options. What did he want? A **ransom**, perhaps? I expected him to say, "Leave two hundred unmarked Milk-Bones in a plain paper bag or you'll never see your precious little necklace again."

"Drop it, Marley," I whispered, taking another small step forward. His whole body began to wag. I crept forward inch by inch. Jenny **closed in** from the side. We were within striking distance. We glanced at each other and knew, without speaking, what to do. We had been through this many times before. She would lunge for the hindquarters, **pin**ning his back legs to prevent escape. I would lunge for the head, prying open his jaws and

---

instinctively 본능적으로 glacier 빙하 wire 연결하다, 묶다 high explosive 고성능 폭탄 set off (폭탄을) 터뜨리다, 자극하다, 작동시키다 ransom 몸값 close in 거리를 좁히다, 접근하다 pin 꼼짝 못하게 붙잡다, 누르다

nabbing the **contraband**. **With any luck**, we'd be in and out in a matter of seconds.

That was the plan, and Marley saw it coming.

We were less than two feet away from him. I **nod**ded to Jenny. "On three," I silently mouthed.

Marley threw his head back and made a loud **smacking** sound. The tail end of the chain, which had been dangling out of his mouth, disappeared.

"He's eating it!" Jenny screamed. Together we **dove at** him. Jenny tackled him by the hind legs. I gripped him **in a headlock**, forced his jaws open, and pushed my whole hand into his mouth and down his throat. I **probe**d every **flap** and **crevice** but came up empty.

"It's too late," I said. "He swallowed it."

"**Cough** it **up**!" Jenny yelled, slapping him on the back.

"Buuuuurrrp!" Marley answered.

Marley may have won the battle, but we knew it was just a matter of time before we won the war. **Nature's call** was on our side. Sooner or later, what went in had to come out. I knew if I **poke**d through his poop long enough, I would find it. It was a disgusting thought, but grossed out or not, I was going in.

---

nab 붙잡다, 낚아채다   contraband 밀수품   with any luck 운이 따라준다면   nod 고개를 끄덕이다   smacking 입맛을 다시는, 짭짭거리는   dive at (~에게) 몸을 날리다, 달려들다, 덮치다   in a headlock 상대의 머리를 팔에 끼어 누르는   probe 살피다   flap 늘어진 부분   crevice 틈새   cough up 기침해서 ~을 토해내다   nature's call 배설 욕구   poke 쿡쿡 찌르다

And so I prepared Marley his favorite **laxative**—a giant bowl of sliced mangoes. Then I settled in for the long wait. For three days I followed him around every time I let him out, eagerly waiting to **swoop in** with my shovel. Instead of tossing his piles over the fence, I carefully placed each on a wide board in the grass. I poked it with a tree branch while I sprayed with a garden hose. The poop washed away into the grass. Anything that wasn't poop stayed behind. I felt like a gold miner coming up with a **treasure trove** of swallowed junk, from shoelaces to guitar picks. But no necklace.

Where was it? Shouldn't it have come out by now? I began wondering if I had missed it, accidentally washing it into the grass. If I had, it would remain lost forever. But how could I miss a twenty-inch gold chain?

On the fourth day, my patience **paid off**.

I scooped up Marley's latest deposit. "I can't believe I'm doing this," I said. I began poking and spraying. As the poop melted away, I searched for any sign of the necklace. Nothing. I was about to give up when I spotted something odd—a small brown lump, about the size of a **lima bean**. It wasn't even close to being large enough

---

laxative 설사제   swoop in 덤벼들다, 급습하다   treasure trove 횡재, 보물   pay off 성과를 내다, 효과를 발휘하다   lima bean 리마콩

to be the missing jewelry, yet clearly it did not seem to belong there. I pinned it down with my probing branch and **gave** the object **a** strong **blast from the hose nozzle**. As the water washed it clean, I got a **glimmer** of something **exceptionally** bright and shiny. Eureka! I had struck gold.

The necklace was much smaller than I would have guessed possible. It was as though some unknown alien power had sucked it into a mysterious **dimension** of space and time before spitting it out again. And, actually, that wasn't too far from the truth. The strong stream of water began to loosen the hard wad, and gradually the lump of gold **unravel**ed back to its original shape, **untangled** and **unmangled**. Good as new. No, actually better than new. I took it inside to show Jenny, who was overjoyed to have it back. She didn't care where it had been. We both **marvel**ed at how **blindingly** bright it was now—far more dazzling than when it had gone in. Marley's stomach acids had done an amazing job. It was the most brilliant gold I had ever seen.

"Man," I said with a whistle. "We should open a jewelry-cleaning business."

---

give a blast from the hose nozzle 호스에서 물줄기를 뿜다 glimmer 희미하게 반짝이는 빛
exceptionally 유난히 dimension 차원 unravel (엉켰던 것이) 풀리다 untangled 엉키지 않은
unmangled 망가지거나 부서지지 않은 marvel 감탄하다 blindingly 눈이 부시게, 매우

"It's got possibilities, Grogan," Jenny said, and went off to **disinfect** her recovered birthday present. She wore that gold chain for years. Every time I looked at it I **had** the same **vivid flashback**. My stick and I had gone where no man had ever gone before. And none should ever go again.

disinfect 소독하다, 세척하다   vivid 생생한, 상세하고 뚜렷한   have a flashback 생생한 기억이 떠오르다

 # Reading Comprehension

1. What was the main reason for why Jenny and John needed to work on Marley's training?

a. There was a baby on the way.
b. They wanted to impress their friends.
c. They were tired of his crazy ways.
d. He was too easily distracted.

2. Complete these sentences with the missing words.

a. Marley ate _____ which made his poop bright orange.
b. The author discovered a shoelace, a rubber band, a soda top bottle and a ballpoint pen cap in Marley's _____.
c. Marley also ate bath towels, sponges, socks and used Kleenex, but _____ were his favorite.
d. Marley always vomited on the _____.

3. Where did Jenny and John find Marley hiding?

a. behind the miniblinds
b. next door at the neighbour's house
c. under the bed
d. in the garage

4. What does the author think of every time he sees his wife wearing the necklace?

a. how shiny and beautiful it is
b. how he had to search for it with a stick through Marley's poop
c. how he should open a jewelry cleaning business
d. how Marley ate it up

 1. a **2.** mangoes, poop, Handi Wipes, fancy rug **3.** c **4.** b

8

The Dog's Got to Go

By 1993, Marley wasn't the only one **keeping us on our toes**. We now also had two human babies—Patrick and Conor. We rarely slept through the night, and Jenny spent her days keeping the boys happy. Between their demands and Marley's **antics**, she was exhausted. Eventually Marley's bad behavior just wasn't funny anymore.

One day I opened the front door to find Jenny crying uncontrollably and **yelling at** Marley.

"Why? Why do you do this?" Jenny screamed at him. "Why do you wreck everything?"

---

keep one on one's toes 긴장을 늦추지 않다 antics 익살스러운 행동 yell at (~에게) 소리를 지르다, 야단치다

In that instant I saw what he had done. The couch cushion was **gouge**d open, the fabric shredded and the **stuffing** pulled out. She was so upset that she started **pound**ing on him with her fists, more like she was beating a **kettledrum** than trying to hurt him. Marley stood with head down and legs spread. He looked as though he was leaning into a hurricane. He didn't try to flee or **dodge** the blows. He just stood there and took each one without a whimper or complaint.

"Hey! Hey! Hey!" I shouted, **grab**bing Jenny's wrists. "Come on. Stop. Stop!" She was **sob**bing and gasping for breath. "Stop," I repeated.

I stepped between her and Marley and shoved my face directly in front of hers. It was like a stranger was staring back at me. I did not recognize the look in her eyes. "Get him out of here," she said, her voice **flat** and **tinged with** a quiet burn. "Get him out of here now."

"Okay, I'll take him out," I said, "but you settle down."

"Get him out of here and keep him out of here," she said.

I opened the front door and he **bound**ed outside. When I turned back to grab his leash off the table, Jenny

---

gouge 후벼 파다, 파헤치다 stuffing 속, 내용물 pound 후려치다, 세게 때리다 kettledrum 케틀드럼 dodge 요리조리 피하다 grab 움켜잡다, 쥐다 sob 흐느껴 울다 flat 맥빠진, 단호한 tinged with (~한) 기색이 보이는 bound 튀어나가다

said, "I mean it. I want him gone. I want him out of here for good."

"Come on," I said. "You don't mean that."

"I mean it," she said. "I'm done with that dog. You find him a new home, or I will."

Jenny couldn't mean it. She loved this dog. She **adore**d him despite his long list of **shortcoming**s. She was upset. She was stressed to the breaking point. She would reconsider. Wouldn't she? One thing was clear—she needed time to **cool down**.

I walked out the door without another word. In the front yard, Marley raced around, jumping into the air and snapping his jaws, trying to bite the leash out of my hand. He was his old **jolly** self. I knew Jenny hadn't hurt him. I **whack**ed him much harder when I played rough with him. He loved it and always bounded back for more. He was an unstoppable machine of muscle and strength that barely felt pain.

Once when I was in the driveway washing the car, he **jam**med his head into the bucket of **soapy** water. He galloped blindly off across the front lawns with the bucket and crashed full force into a concrete wall. It

---

adore 아끼다, 귀여워하다   shortcoming 단점   cool down 진정하다   jolly 유쾌한, 명랑한   whack 세게 치다, 퍽 소리가 나게 때리다   jam 쑤셔 넣다   soapy 비누가 녹은

didn't seem to faze him.

Even though he was a big dense **oaf**, Marley did have an incredibly sensitive **streak**. If someone got angry and slapped him lightly on the **rump** or even just spoke to him with a stern voice, he acted deeply wounded.

Jenny hadn't hurt Marley physically, not even close, but she had **crush**ed his feelings. One of his two best **pal**s in the whole world had just turned on him. She was his **mistress** and he was her faithful companion. He figured that if she needed to strike him, he needed to **suck** it **up** and take it. As far as dogs went, he was not good at much. But he was unquestionably loyal. Now it was my job to repair the damage and make things right again.

Out on the street, I hooked him to his leash. "Sit!" I ordered. He sat. I pulled the choke chain up high on his throat in preparation for our walk. Before I stepped off I ran my hand over his head and massaged his neck. He **flip**ped his nose in the air and looked up at me, his tongue hanging halfway down his neck. He had forgotten all about what had happened with Jenny. I hoped she had, too.

"What am I going to do with you, you big **dope**?" I

---

oaf 저능아, 멍청이 streak 측면, 양상 rump (짐승의) 둔부, 엉덩이 crush 뭉개다, 짓밟다 pal 친구, 동무
mistress 개의 여주인 suck up 감내하다 flip 확 움직이다 dope 멍청이

asked him. He leaped straight up, as though he had **spring**s on his **paw**s, and **smash**ed his tongue against my lips.

Marley and I walked for miles that evening, and when I finally opened the front door, he was exhausted and ready to collapse quietly in the corner. Jenny was feeding Patrick a jar of baby food as she **cradle**d Conor in her **lap**. She was calm. *Whew!* I thought. Back to her old self.

I unleashed Marley, and he took a huge drink. Water **slosh**ed like little **tidal wave**s over the side of his bowl. I toweled up the floor and stole a glance in Jenny's direction. She didn't seem upset at all. Maybe the horrible moment had passed. Maybe she had reconsidered. Maybe she felt **sheepish** about her **outburst** and was searching for the words to apologize. I walked past her, with Marley close at my heels.

"I'm **dead** serious," she said without looking at me. "I want him out of here."

I was not ready to give up on Marley.

To make Jenny happy, I started looking for a new home for him. At the same time, I began the most serious training Marley had ever gotten. My own private Mission: Impossible was to **rehabilitate** this dog and prove to

spring 용수철 paw 동물의 발 smash 강타하다 cradle 품에 안다, 보듬다 lap 무릎 slosh 찰랑거리다
tidal wave 큰 파도, 해일 sheepish 멋쩍어하는, 부끄러워하는 outburst 격분 dead 완전히, 전적으로
rehabilitate (~의) 명예를 회복시키다, 원상복귀시키다

Jenny he was worthy. I began rising at dawn. With Patrick in the **jogging stroller**, I headed down to the water to **put Marley through the paces**.

Sit. Stay. Down. Heel. Over and over we practiced. I was desperate, and Marley seemed to sense it. The **stake**s were different now—this was for real.

"We're not **messing around** here, Marley," I told him. "This is it. Let's go." And I put him through the commands again.

"Waddy! Hee-O!" Patrick clapped and called to his big yellow friend.

I couldn't do it alone. I reenrolled Marley in obedience school. He was a different dog from the **juvenile delinquent** I had shown up with the first time around. He was still as wild as a **boar**, but this time he knew I was the boss and he was the **underling**. This time there would be no lunges toward other dogs—or at least not many. No out-of-control **surge**s across the tarmac. No **crashing into** strangers.

For eight weeks I kept him on a tight leash and marched him through the commands. He was overjoyed to cooperate.

---

stroller 유모차   jogging stroller 조깅 유모차   put someone through their paces 역량을 시험하다   stake (계획, 행동의 성공 여부에) 걸려 있는 것, 관심사나 관련성   mess around 빈둥대다   juvenile delinquent 비행 청소년   boar 멧돼지   underling 부하   surge 돌진, 쇄도   crash into 충돌하다

The trainer was the exact opposite of the first instructor we had had. At our final meeting, she called us forward. "Okay," she said, "show us what you've got."

"Sit," I ordered. Marley dropped neatly to his **backside**. I raised the choker chain high around his throat and tugged on his lead. "Heel!" I commanded. I trotted across the parking lot and back with Marley at my side. His shoulder brushed my calf, just as it was supposed to.

"Sit," I ordered again. I stood directly in front of him and pointed my finger at his forehead. "Stay," I said calmly. With the other hand I dropped his leash. I stepped backward several paces. His big brown eyes fixed on me, waiting for any small sign from me to release him, but he remained anchored. I walked in a circle around him. He **quiver**ed with excitement and tried to rotate his head to watch me, but he did not budge.

When I was back in front of him, I decided to have a little fun. I snapped my fingers and yelled, "Incoming!" He hit the deck. The teacher burst out laughing. That was a good sign. I turned my back on him and walked thirty feet away. I could feel his eyes burning into my back, but he didn't move. He was quaking violently by the time

backside 엉덩이, 둔부 **quiver** 달달 떨다

I turned around to face him. Marley the Volcano was getting ready to blow.

I spread my feet into a wide boxer's **stance** in anticipation of what was coming. "Marley . . . ," I said. I let his name hang in the air for a few seconds. "Come!" He shot at me with everything he had, and I **braced for** the impact. At the last instant I stepped to the side like a bullfighter. He **blast**ed past me, then circled back and **goose**d me from behind with his nose.

"Good boy, Marley," I **gush**ed, dropping to my knees. "Good, good, good boy! You're a good boy!" He danced around me like we had just climbed to the top of Mount Everest together.

At the end of the evening, the instructor called us up and handed us our **diploma**. Marley had passed basic obedience training, **rank**ing seventh in the class. So what if it was a class of eight and the eighth dog was a crazy pit bull? I would take it. Marley, my untrainable, undisciplined bad-boy dog, had passed. I was so proud I could have cried. In fact I actually might have had Marley not leaped up and eaten his diploma.

On the way home, I sang "We Are the Champions" at

---

stance 선 자세 brace for 대비하다 blast 쏜살같이 달려가다, 질주하다 goose 똥침을 놓다 gush 과장된 말투로 칭찬을 늘어놓다 diploma 수료증 rank (~번째) 순위에 오르다

the top of my lungs. Sensing my joy and pride, Marley stuck his **slimy** tongue in my ear. For once, I didn't even mind.

slimy 끈적끈적한, 질척한

Reading Comprehension

1. What did Jenny ask John to do with Marley?

a. to take Marley for a long walk
b. to punish Marley for being naughty
c. to get rid of Marley permanently
d. to take Marley to obedience school

2. What hurt Marley the most?

a. rejection from his owner
b. being hit with a stick
c. being choked by a chain
d. being replaced by the babies

3. Which of these was not part of the author's plan to rehabilitate Marley?

a. training Marley to obey his commands
b. enrolling Marley in obedience school
c. being disciplined for eight weeks
d. feeding him a diploma to cure him of naughtiness

4. Which of these best describes the author's feelings about Marley finishing obedience school?

a. overwhelmed and relieved
b. proud and triumphant
c. sad and tearful
d. amazed and shocked

Answers: **1.** c **2.** a **3.** d **4.** b

9

The Final Round

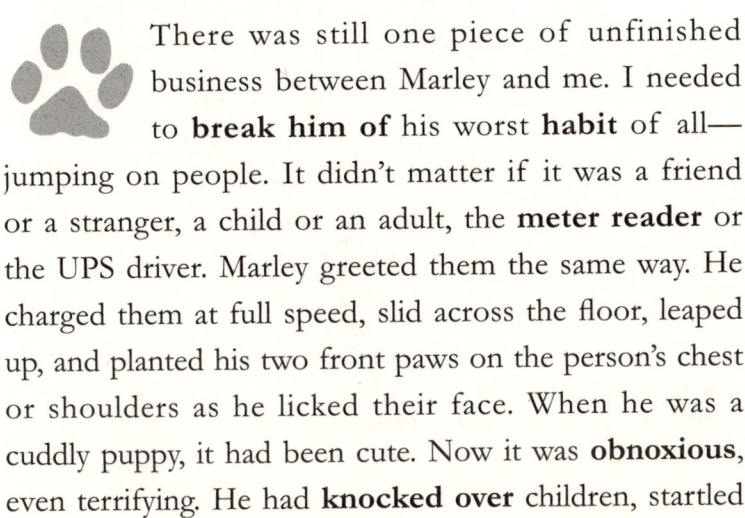There was still one piece of unfinished business between Marley and me. I needed to **break him of** his worst **habit** of all—jumping on people. It didn't matter if it was a friend or a stranger, a child or an adult, the **meter reader** or the UPS driver. Marley greeted them the same way. He charged them at full speed, slid across the floor, leaped up, and planted his two front paws on the person's chest or shoulders as he licked their face. When he was a cuddly puppy, it had been cute. Now it was **obnoxious**, even terrifying. He had **knocked over** children, startled

break someone of habit 버릇을 고쳐주다   meter reader 계량기 검침원   obnoxious 불쾌한, 못된
knock over 치거나 부딪혀서 넘어뜨리다

guests, dirtied our friends' clothes, and nearly **taken down** my **frail** mother. No one appreciated it.

Although I had tried breaking him of his habit, regular dog-obedience techniques hadn't worked. The message was not **getting through**.

"You want to break him of that?" a dog owner I respected asked. "**Give him a** swift **knee** in the chest next time he jumps up on you."

"I don't want to hurt him," I said.

"You won't hurt him. A few good jabs with your knee, and I guarantee you he'll be done jumping."

It was **tough-love** time. Marley had to reform or **relocate**.

I put my plan into action the next night. "I'm home!" I yelled when I walked in from work.

As usual, Marley came barreling across the wood floors to greet me. He slid the last ten feet as though on ice. Then he lifted off to smash his paws into my chest and **slurp** at my face.

Bam! Just as his paws made contact with me, I **gave one swift pump of my knee**. I aimed for the soft spot just below his rib cage. Marley gasped slightly and slid

---

take down 쓰러뜨리다, 넘어뜨리다   frail 허약한, 연약한   get through 전달되다   give someone a knee 무릎으로 치다   tough-love 사랑의 매, 사랑하는 사람을 위해 취하는 매정한 태도   relocate 보금자리를 옮기다, 다른 곳으로 떠나다   slurp 짭짭거리는 소리를 내다   give one swift pump of one's knee 무릎을 재빨리 한 번 위로 들어 올리다

down to the floor, looking up at me with a wounded expression.

"What's your problem?" I could almost hear him say. He had been jumping on me his whole life. What was with the sudden **sneak** attack?

The next night I repeated the punishment. He leaped. I kneed. He dropped to the floor, coughing. I felt a little cruel, but if I was going to save him, I knew I had to **drive home the point**.

"Sorry, guy," I said, leaning down so he could lick me with all four paws on the ground. "It's for your own good."

The third night when I walked in, he came charging around the corner, going into his high-speed **skid**. This time, however, he changed the routine. Instead of leaping, he kept his paws on the ground and crashed headfirst into my knees, nearly knocking me over. Yes! Victory!

"You did it, Marley! You did it! Good boy! You didn't jump up," I praised. And I got on my knees so he could slobber me. I was impressed.

The problem was not exactly solved, however. He may

---

sneak 느닷없는, 예고 없이 일어나는　drive home the point 중요한 점을 짚고 넘어가다, 분명히 하다　skid 미끄럼

have been cured of jumping on me, but he was not cured of jumping on anyone else. The dog was smart enough to figure out that only I posed a threat. He could still jump on the rest of the human race. I needed a plan.

I asked a good friend of mine from work to help me out. Jim Tolpin was a small, mild-mannered man with glasses. If there was anyone Marley thought he could jump up on **without consequence**, it was Jim.

At the office one day, I **laid out the plan**. He was to come to the house after work, ring the doorbell, and then walk in. When Marley jumped up to kiss him, he was to give him all he had. "Don't be shy about it," I coached.

That night Jim rang the bell and walked in the door. Sure enough, Marley **took the bait** and raced at him, ears flying back. When Marley left the ground to leap up on him, Jim took my advice to heart. He kneed Marley right in the soft spot below his ribs, **knocking the wind out of** him. You could hear the thud across the room. Marley let out a loud moan, went **bug-eyed**, and sprawled on the floor.

"Have you been studying kung fu?" I asked.

"You told me to make him feel it," he answered.

---

without consequence 앞뒤 가리지 않고   lay out a plan 계획을 세우다   take the bait 미끼를 물다
knock the wind out of 세게 쳐서 숨이 막히게 하다   bug-eyed (놀라서) 눈이 휘둥그러진

He had. Marley got to his feet, **caught his breath**, and greeted Jim the way a dog should—on all four paws. If he could have talked, I swear Marley would have **cried "Uncle."** Marley never again jumped up on anyone, at least not in my presence, and no one ever kneed him in the chest or anywhere else again.

Gradually Jenny found it in her heart to forgive Marley for all his **misdeed**s. One morning she woke up and it was like she had completely forgotten about her threat to send him away. With a baby in each arm, Jenny leaned to kiss him. She threw him sticks and made him **gravy** from hamburger drippings. She danced him around the room when a good song came on the stereo. Sometimes at night when he was calm, I would find her lying on the floor with him, her head resting on his neck.

Our new and improved dog was here to stay.

catch one's breath 놀라서 숨이 막히다, 헐떡이다 cry uncle 항복하다 misdeed 나쁜 짓, 비행 gravy 육즙으로 만든 소스

Reading Comprehension

1. Match the reaction of each person to Marley's greeting.

a. Children
b. Guests
c. Friends
d. Mother

1) They were startled.
2) She was nearly taken down.
3) Their clothes got dirty.
4) They were knocked over.

2. Put these sentences in the right order.

a. Marley greets John by jumping up on him.
b. John asks Jim to knee Marley in the chest.
c. Marley no longer jumps on people to greet them.
d. John knees him in the chest.

3. What was Marley's reaction to being kneed in the chest?

a. He was seriously wounded.
b. He was surprised and shocked.
c. He was sad and upset.
d. He was happy and undeterred.

4. Which of these was not how Jenny expressed her love for Marley again?

a. She kneed him in the chest.
b. She kissed him.
c. She made him gravy.
d. She danced with him.

Answers: **1.** a-4, b-1, c-3, d-2 **2.** a-d-b-c **3.** b **4.** a

10

The Audition

Some things in life are so **weird** they have to be true. So when Jenny called me at the office to tell me Marley was getting a film **audition**, I knew she couldn't be making it up. Still, I was in disbelief.

"A what?" I asked.

"A film audition."

"Like for a movie?"

"Yes, like for a movie, dumbo," she said. "A **feature-length movie**."

"Marley? A feature-length movie? Our Marley?" I asked

---

weird 이상한, 괴상한   audition 오디션   feature-length movie 장편 상업 영화

one more time, just to be sure.

It had all started out very simple. A New York film company was making a movie and wanted to see how a typical Florida family lived. They asked if they could photograph our home.

A woman named Colleen came over and started photographing. She took pictures of *everything*—the way we dressed, the way we wore our hair, the way we **slouch**ed on the couch. She photographed toothbrushes on the sink. She photographed the babies in their **crib**s. She photographed our dog, too. Or at least what she could catch of him on film.

"He's a bit of a **blur**," she said.

Marley could not have been happier to participate. Ever since babies had **invade**d, Marley ate up all the affection he could get. Colleen could have **jab**bed him with a **cattle prod**. As long as he was getting some attention, he was okay with it. Being a lover of large animals and not intimidated by **saliva** showers, Colleen gave him plenty. She dropped to her knees to wrestle with him.

When she was done, Colleen thanked us and left. We didn't expect to hear from her again. Our job was done.

---

slouch 구부정하게 앉거나 서다 crib 요람, 아기용 침대 blur (빨리 움직여서) 모양이 불분명한 형체 invade 침략하다, 자리를 빼앗다 jab 쿡 찌르다 cattle prod 소몰이 막대 saliva 침

A few days later Jenny called me at work. "I just got off the phone with Colleen McGarr," she said. "You are NOT going to believe it."

"Go on," I said.

"She says the director wants Marley to try out," Jenny said.

"Marley?" I asked, certain I had **misheard**. She didn't seem to notice the dismay in my voice.

"Apparently, he's looking for a big, dumb, **loopy** dog to play the role of the family pet," she explained. "Marley **caught his eye**."

"Loopy?" I asked.

"That's what Colleen says he wants. Big, dumb, and loopy."

Well, he had certainly come to the right place.

Colleen picked up Marley the next day. Knowing the importance of a **good entrance**, he came racing through the living room to greet her at full speed, pausing only long enough to grab the nearest pillow in his teeth. (You never knew when a busy film director might need a quick nap, and if he did, I guess Marley wanted to be ready.)

When he hit the wood floor, he flew into a full skid. He

---

mishear 잘못 듣다 loopy 미친, 괴상한 catch someone's eye (~의) 눈에 띄다, 마음에 들다 good entrance 순조로운 출발, 첫 단추를 잘 끼우기

didn't stop until he hit the coffee table, went **airborne**, crashed into a chair, landed on his back, rolled, scrambled back to his feet, and collided head-on into Colleen's legs.

At least he didn't jump up, I noted.

Colleen drove off in her red pickup truck with our desperately happy dog beside her.

Two hours later Colleen and **Company** were back. The **verdict** was in—Marley had passed the audition.

"Oh, shut up!" Jenny shrieked. "No way!"

I asked her how the audition went.

"I got Marley in the car and it was like driving in a **Jacuzzi**," she said. "He was slobbering on everything. By the time I got him there, I was **drench**ed."

They arrived at production **headquarters** at the Gulf Stream Hotel a few miles from our house. Marley immediately impressed the crew by jumping out of the truck and **tear**ing around the parking lot in random patterns. He moved like he expected bombs to start dropping at any moment.

"He was just **berserk**, completely **mental**," Colleen **recount**ed.

"Yeah, he gets a little excited," I said.

---

airborne 공중으로, 날아서 company 일행, 일당 verdict 평가, 의견 Jacuzzi 기포 욕조 drench 흠뻑 적시다 headquarters 본부 tear 날뛰다 berserk 광포한 mental 미친 recount 이야기하다, 설명하다

"At one point, Marley grabbed the **checkbook** out of a crew member's hand and raced away," she explained. "He ran around in a bunch of tight **figure eight**s to nowhere."

"We call him our Labrador evader," Jenny apologized. Then she made the kind of smile only a proud mother can make.

Marley eventually calmed down enough to convince everyone he could do the part, which was basically to just play himself. The movie was called *The Last Home Run.* In it, a seventy-nine-year-old man becomes a twelve-year-old for five days to live his dream of playing Little League ball. Marley was **cast** as the hyperactive family dog of the Little League coach, played by retired major-league catcher Gary Carter.

"They really want him to be in their movie?" I asked.

"Everyone loved him," Colleen said. "He's perfect." She explained that he wouldn't get paid, but I didn't care. My dog was going to be a star!

In the days leading up to shooting, we noticed a change in Marley's behavior. A strange **calm** had come over him. It was as if passing the audition had given him

---

checkbook 수표책   figure eight 8자 모양   cast ~을 캐스팅하다   in the days leading up to something ~이 얼마 남지 않았을 때   shooting 촬영   calm 침착함, 평정

new confidence. He was almost **regal**.

"Maybe he just needed someone to believe in him," I told Jenny.

If anyone believed, it was her, **Stage Mom Extraordinaire**. As the first day of filming approached, she bathed him. She brushed him. She **clip**ped his nails and **swab**bed out his ears.

On the morning shooting was to begin, I walked out of the bedroom to find Jenny and Marley **tangle**d together. They seemed to be locked in **mortal** combat, bouncing across the room. She was **straddling** him like a horse, with her knees tightly hugging his ribs. One hand grasped the end of his choker chain as he **buck**ed and lurched. It was like having a rodeo right in my own living room.

"What on earth are you doing?" I asked.

"What's it look like?" she shot back. "Brushing his teeth!"

Sure enough, Jenny had a toothbrush in the other hand and was doing her best to scrub his big white **ivories**. **Froth**ing at the mouth, Marley did his best to eat the toothbrush. He looked **positively rabid**.

"Are you using toothpaste?" I asked.

---

regal 제왕다운, 위풍당당한 stage mom 자식을 배우나 모델을 시키려는 극성 엄마 extraordinaire (뒤에서 수식함) 최고의 clip 깎다, 자르다 swab (~을) 닦다, 청소하다 tangle 뒤엉키다 mortal 생사를 건, 치명적인 straddle 다리를 넓게 벌린 채 (~위에) 서거나 앉다 buck 껑충껑충 뛰다, 날뛰다 ivories 이, 치아 froth 거품을 물다 positively 완전히 rabid 광견병에 걸린, 미친

"Baking soda," she answered.

"Thank goodness," I said. "So it's *not* rabies?"

An hour later, we left for the Gulf Stream Hotel. The boys sat in their car seats with Marley between them, **pant**ing away with abnormally fresh breath. Colleen had told us to arrive by 9:00 A.M., but a block away, traffic came to a **standstill**. Up ahead, the road was barricaded and a police officer was **divert**ing traffic away from the hotel. The movie was the biggest event to hit the town in fifteen years, and a crowd of spectators had turned out to **gawk**. The police were keeping everyone away.

We **inch**ed forward in traffic. When we finally got up to the officer I leaned out the window and said, "We need to get through."

"No one gets through," he said. "Keep moving. Let's go."

"We're with the cast," I said.

The officer eyed us skeptically—a couple in a minivan with two **toddler**s and the family pet. "I said move it!" he **bark**ed.

"Our dog is in the film," I said.

Suddenly he looked at me with new respect. "You have

---

pant 헐떡이다 **standstill** 정지, 정체 **divert** 방향을 돌리게 하다, 우회시키다 **gawk** 멍하니 바라보다 **inch** 느릿느릿 움직이다, 기어가다 **toddler** 걸음마를 시작한 아이 **bark** 사납게 소리치다, 딱딱거리다

the dog?" he asked. The dog was on his **checklist**.

"I have the dog," I said. "Marley the Dog."

"Playing himself," Jenny **chimed in**.

He turned around and blew his whistle **with** great **fanfare**. "He's got the dog!" he shouted to a cop a half block down. "Marley the Dog!"

And that cop yelled to someone else, "He's got the dog! Marley the Dog's here!"

"Let 'em through!" a third officer shouted from the distance.

"Let 'em through!" the second cop **echo**ed.

The officer moved the barricade and waved us through. "Right this way," he said politely. I felt like **royalty**. As we rolled past him he said once again, as if he could not quite believe it, "He's got the dog."

In the parking lot outside the hotel, the film **crew** was ready for action. Cables **crisscross**ed the pavement. Camera **tripod**s and **microphone boom**s were set up. Lights hung from **scaffolding**. Trailers held **rack**s of costumes. Two large tables of food and drinks were set up in the shade for cast and crew. Important-looking people in sunglasses **bustle**d about.

---

checklist 목록, 점검표　chime in 끼어들어 말하다, 장단을 맞추다　with fanfare 요란하게　echo 반복하다　royalty 왕족　crew 직원, 스태프　crisscross 십자로 교차하다, 엇갈리다　tripod 삼각대　microphone boom 마이크를 매다는 틀　scaffolding 가설물　rack 옷걸이　bustle 부산을 떨다, 바삐 움직이다

The director greeted us and gave us a quick **rundown** of Marley's scene. It went like this: A minivan pulls up to the curb. Marley's **make-believe** owner is **at the wheel**. Her daughter and son are in the back with their family dog, played by Marley. The daughter opens the sliding door and hops out. Her brother follows with Marley on a leash. They **walk off** camera. End of scene.

"Easy enough," I told the director. "He should be able to handle that, no problem." I pulled Marley off to the side to wait for his **cue** to get into the van.

"Okay, people, listen up," the director told the crew. "The dog's a little **nutty**, okay? But unless he completely **hijack**s the scene, we're going to keep **roll**ing. Just let him do his thing," he coached, "and work around him."

When everyone was set to go, I **load**ed Marley into the van and handed his nylon leash to the little boy, who looked terrified. "He's friendly," I told him. "He'll just want to lick you. See?" I stuck my wrist in Marley's mouth to demonstrate.

When filming started, the scene turned out to be a little trickier than I'd expected. The reason was simple— Marley.

rundown 요약, 간략한 설명 make-believe (~인) 척 하는, 가공의 at the wheel 운전대 앞에 앉은, 운전 중인 walk off (~의) 바깥으로 걸어나가다 cue 큐 신호 nutty 미친, 정신이 없는 hijack 제멋대로 휘젓다 roll 계속하다, 진행하다 load 싣다

Take one. The van pulls to the curb. The daughter slides open the side door. A yellow streak shoots out. Like a giant **furball** being fired from a **cannon**, it **blur**s past the cameras.

"Cut!" the director shouted.

I chased Marley down in the parking lot and **haul**ed him back.

"Okay, folks, we're going to try that again," the director said. Then, to the boy, he coached gently, "The dog's pretty wild. Try to hold on tighter this time."

Take two. The van pulls to the curb. The door slides open. The daughter is just beginning to exit when Marley **huff**s into view and leaps out past her. This time he drags the **white-knuckled** and white-faced boy behind him.

"Cut!" the director shouted.

Take three. The van pulls up. The door slides open. The daughter exits. The boy exits, holding the leash. As he steps away from the van the leash pulls **taut**, but no dog follows. The boy begins to tug, heave, and pull. He leans into it and gives it everything he has. Not a **budge**. Long, painful seconds pass. The boy **grimace**s and looks back at the camera.

---

furball 털 뭉치   cannon 대포   blur 흐릿해지다   haul 질질 끌고 가다   huff 헐떡거리다   white-knuckled 겁에 질린   taut 팽팽하게 당겨진   budge 움직임   grimace 인상을 쓰다

"Cut!" the director shouted.

I peered into the van to find Marley bent over, licking himself. He looked up at me as if to say, "Can't you see I'm busy?"

Take four. I load Marley into the back of the van with the boy and shut the door. The van pulls to the curb. The door slides open. The daughter steps out. The boy steps out—with a **bewildered** look on his face. He peers directly into the camera and holds up his hand. Dangling from it is half the leash. The end is **jagged** and wet with saliva.

"Cut! Cut! Cut!" the director shouted.

The boy explained that as he waited in the van, Marley began gnawing on the leash and wouldn't stop. The crew and cast were staring at the severed leash in disbelief. A mix of **awe** and horror formed on their faces. It was like nothing they'd ever seen. I, on the other hand, was not surprised in the least. Marley had destroyed more leashes and ropes than I could remember.

"Okay, everybody, let's take a break," the director called out. He turned to me and asked in an amazingly calm voice, "How quickly can you find a new leash?" I knew

---

bewildered 당황한, 어쩔 줄 모르는   jagged 들쭉날쭉하게 잘린   awe 경외감

that every minute cost big money.

"There's a pet store a half mile from here," I said. "I can be back in fifteen minutes."

"And this time get something he can't chew through," he said.

I returned with a heavy chain leash that looked like something a lion trainer might use. The filming continued, but each scene was worse than the one before. At one point, the actress who played the daughter let out a desperate **shriek** midscene and screamed with true horror in her voice, "Oh, no! His **thing** is out!"

"Cut!" the director shouted.

That's how Day One of shooting went. Marley was a **disaster**—a complete and total disaster. Part of me was defensive. *Well, what did they expect for free? Benji?* Part was **mortified**. I glanced at the cast and crew. The looks on their faces screamed, "Where did this animal come from, and how can we send him back?"

"**Don't bother coming** in tomorrow," one of the assistants told us at the end of the day. "We'll call if we need Marley." To make sure there was no confusion, he repeated, "So unless you hear from us, don't show up.

---

shriek 날카로운 비명   thing 그것, 거시기   disaster 골칫덩이   mortify 모욕을 주다, 창피를 주다   don't bother doing 굳이 ~하지 마시오, 굳이 ~하지 않아도 좋다

Got it?"

Yeah, I got it, loud and clear. The director had sent his assistant to do the **dirty work**.

Marley's acting career was over. Not that I could blame them. Marley had been a nightmare. Thanks to him, thousands of dollars had been wasted. He had **slime**d countless costumes, **raid**ed the snack table, and nearly knocked over a $30,000 camera. It was the old "don't call us, we'll call you" **routine**.

"Marley," I said when we got home, "your big chance and you really **blew** it."

---

dirty work 곤란한/난처한 일　slime (~에) 침을 바르다　raid 급습하다, 덮치다　routine 관습적인/의례적인 절차　blow (기회 따위를) 망치다, 날려버리다

Reading Comprehension

1. Why did Colleen wish to photograph the Grogan's house?

a. She wanted to take photos of Marley the famous dog.
b. She wanted to find out how a typical family in Florida lived.
c. She wanted to publish the photos in a dog magazine.
d. She was hired by the Grogans to take family photos.

2. Which of these does not mean the same as "crazy"?

a. loopy   b. berserk   c. regal   d. nutty

3. The following passage describes how Jenny cleaned Marley. Fill in the blanks with the following words.

a. clipped   b. brushed   c. teeth   d. swabbed

Jenny _____ his fur and _____ his nails. She bathed him, and _____ his ears. She also tried to brush his _____.

4. Match the take number with Marley's actions that ruined the scene.

a. Take one (   )   b. Take two (   )
c. Take three (   )   d. Take four (   )

1) The van door opens but Marley has chewed the leash in half.
2) The van door opens but Marley is still inside licking himself.
3) As the van door opens, Marley runs out like a blurry streak.
4) As the van door opens, Marley runs out, dragging the boy behind him.

Answers: **1.** b **2.** c **3.** b-a-d-c **4.** a-3, b-4, c-2, d-1

11

Take Two

 The next morning the phone rang. It was the assistant, telling us to get Marley to the hotel as soon as possible.

"You mean you want him back?" I asked.

"Right away," he said. "The director wants him in the next scene."

I arrived thirty minutes later, still not quite believing they had invited us back. The director was all **fired up**. He had watched the **raw footage** from the day before and could not have been happier.

"The dog was **hysterical**!" he gushed. "Just **hilarious**.

---

fired up 열의가 넘치는, 고무된 **raw** 편집하지 않은 원래 상태의 **footage** 촬영된 필름의 일부분, 촬영분
hysterical 배꼽을 빼게 만드는, 매우 웃긴 **hilarious** 웃게 만드는, 매우 웃긴

Pure **madcap** genius!" I could feel myself standing taller, chest **puffing out**.

"We always knew he was **a natural**," Jenny said.

Shooting continued for several more days, and Marley continued to **rise to the occasion**. He was **lapping up stardom**. The crew, especially the women, **fawned over** him. The weather was brutally hot, and one assistant had to follow Marley around with a bowl and a bottle of spring water, pouring him drinks whenever he wanted. Everyone, it seemed, was feeding him snacks off the buffet table.

I left him with the crew for a couple hours while I checked in at work. When I returned, I found him **sprawl**ed out like **King Tut**, paws in the air, accepting a **leisurely** belly rub from the makeup artist. "He's such a lover!" she **coo**ed.

Stardom was starting to go to my head, too. I began introducing myself as "Marley the Dog's **handler**." I dropped lines such as, "For his next movie, we're hoping for a barking part."

During one break in the shooting, I walked into the hotel lobby to use the pay phone. Marley was off his

---

madcap 덤벙대는. 천방지축의 puff out 부풀다 a natural 재능을 타고난 사람이나 것 rise to the occasion 고비를 잘 넘기다. 임무를 성공적으로 해내다 lap up (관심이나 귀빈 대접을) 즐기다. 누리다 stardom 스타의 지위, 신분 fawn over (~에게) 비위를 맞추다. 아양을 떨다 sprawl 사지를 쭉 뻗고 퍼져 눕거나 앉다 King Tut 투탕카멘 leisurely 여유로운, 느긋한 coo 애정 어린 목소리로 말하다 handler 조련사

leash and sniffing around the furniture several feet away. A **concierge**, apparently mistaking my star for a **stray**, tried to **hustle** him out a side door.

"Go home!" he scolded. "Shoo!"

"Excuse me?" I said, **cupping my hand over** the mouthpiece of the phone and **shooting** him my most **withering stare**. "Do you have any idea who you're talking to?"

We remained on the set for four straight days. But it was two full years later before I finally got my chance to see Marley's acting skills.

I was in Blockbuster when **on a whim** I asked the clerk if he knew anything about a movie called *The Last Home Run*. He knew about it *and* he had it in stock. In fact, as luck would have it, not a single copy was **checked out**.

I raced home with a copy and yelled to Jenny and the kids to gather around the VCR. Marley was on screen for less than two minutes. But they were definitely two of the livelier minutes in the film. We laughed! We cried! We cheered!

"Waddy, that you!" Conor screamed.

"We're famous!" Patrick yelled.

---

concierge 호텔의 접수계원 stray 떠돌이 동물 hustle 밀어내다, 쫓아내다 cup one's hand over 손으로 (~을) 막다, 덮다 withering 위압적인, 기죽게 하는 shoot a withering stare 매섭게 쏘아보다, 따가운 눈총을 주다 on a whim 즉흥적으로, 충동적으로 check out 대출하다, 빌리다

Marley yawned and **crawl**ed under the coffee table. By the end of the movie, he was sound asleep. We held our breath and waited to see his name in the credits. For a while, I thought they were going to leave him out. But then there it was, listed in big letters across the screen for all to see.

MARLEY THE DOG . . . AS HIMSELF.

crawl 기어가다

Reading Comprehension

1. Why did the director ask Marley to come back?

a. He couldn't find another dog to replace Marley.
b. He was desperate to finish shooting the movie.
c. The author begged the director to take Marley back.
d. He had watched the footage and thought Marley was so funny.

2. Which of the following did Marley least enjoy about shooting the movie?

a. getting fed snacks from the table by the crew
b. getting a belly rub from the make up artist
c. watching his two minutes on screen in the movie at home
d. getting drinks poured for him whenever he wanted

3. How did John feel about Marley's acting in the movie?

a. proud and superior
b. humble and honored
c. happy and overjoyed
d. excited and nervous

4. What was Marley labeled as in the credits?

a. Marley the dog as himself
b. Mambo Marley the dog as himself
c. The dog as Marley
d. Crazy Marley the dog as himself

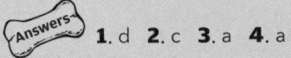

Answers: **1.** d **2.** c **3.** a **4.** a

12

Jail Break

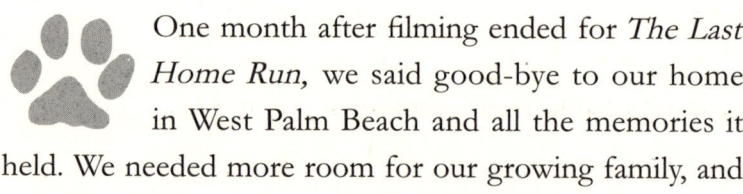 One month after filming ended for *The Last Home Run,* we said good-bye to our home in West Palm Beach and all the memories it held. We needed more room for our growing family, and we moved into a new house in Boca Raton.

From our living-room window we could see a small city park filled with playground equipment. The kids adored it. And our new house had an **inground** swimming pool.

No one loved the pool more than our water dog. If the pool gate was open, Marley would charge for the water. Getting a running start from the family room, he flew out

inground 땅을 파서 만든

the open doors. With one bounce off the brick **patio**, he'd land in the pool on his belly **with a giant flop** that sent a **geyser** into the air and waves over the edge.

Swimming with Marley was potentially life threatening, a little like swimming with an ocean **liner**. He would come at you full speed ahead, his paws flailing out in front of him. You'd expect him to veer away at the last minute, but he would simply crash into you and try to climb aboard. If you were over your head, he could push you beneath the surface.

"What do I look like, a **dock**?" I would say, and cradle him in my arms to let him **catch his breath**. His front paws **paddle**d away on **autopilot** as he licked the water off my face.

One thing our new house did not have was a **Marley-proof** bunker. At our old house, the concrete one-car garage was pretty much indestructible, and it had two windows that kept it comfortable even **in the dead of summer**. Our Boca house had a two-car garage, but it had no windows and was **stiflingly** hot. Sometimes the temperature felt like 150 degrees. We needed to find a place for him in the house.

---

patio 테라스 with a giant flop 요란하게 풍덩/철썩 소리를 내며 geyser 간헐 온천 liner 정기선, 대형 여객선 dock 부두 catch one's breath 한숨 돌리다, 가쁜 숨을 가라앉히다 paddle 물 속에서 걷는 것처럼 물을 휘젓다 autopilot 자동 조종 장치 Marley-proof 말리를 견뎌낼/감당할 수 있는 in the dead of summer 한여름에 stiflingly 숨 막히게

The first time we left him alone in our new house, we shut him in the laundry room, just off the kitchen, with a blanket and a big bowl of water. When we returned a few hours later, he had scratched up the door. The damage was minor, but we knew it was a bad sign, considering his horrible fear of thunder.

"Maybe he's just getting used to his new surroundings," I offered.

"There's not even a cloud in the sky," Jenny observed skeptically. "What's going to happen the first time a storm hits?"

The next time we left him alone, we found out. As **thunderhead**s rolled in, we **cut** our **outing short** and hurried home. It was too late. Jenny was a few steps ahead of me. She opened the laundry-room door.

"Oh my goodness." She said it the way you would if you had just entered a crime scene. Again: "Oh . . . my . . . goodness."

I **peek**ed in over her shoulder, and it was worse than I had feared. Marley was standing there, panting frantically, his paws and mouth bleeding. Loose fur was everywhere, as though the thunder had scared the hair right out of his

---

thunderhead 소나기구름 **cut short** 일찍 끝내다, 줄이다 **outing** 외출, 나들이 **peek** 훔쳐 보다, 엿보다

coat. The damage was worse than anything he had ever done before, and that was saying a lot. An entire wall was gouged open. Plaster and wood chips and bent nails were everywhere. Electric wiring lay exposed. Blood smeared the floor and the walls.

"Oh my goodness," Jenny said a third time.

"Oh my goodness," I repeated. It was all either of us could say.

"Okay, we can handle this. It's all fixable," I said, after several seconds of just standing there **mute**.

"A few hundred bucks and we'll be good as new," she **chirp**ed.

"That's what I'm thinking, too," I said.

As we talked, Marley **curled up** on the rug in front of the kitchen sink and let out a deep sigh. I **knelt** beside him and **stroke**d his **blood-caked** fur. "Geez, dog," I said. "What are we going to do with you?" Without lifting his head, he looked up at me with the saddest, most mournful eyes I have ever seen, and just gazed at me. It was as if he were trying to tell me something, something important he needed me to understand.

"I know," I said. "I know you can't help it."

---

mute 말문이 막힌 채, 아무 말도 못한 채   chirp 명랑하게 말하다   curl up 몸을 둥그렇게 말다, 웅크리다
kneel 무릎을 꿇고 앉다   stroke 어루만지다, 쓰다듬다   blood-caked 피투성이가 된, 피딱지가 앉은

The next day Jenny and I took the boys with us to the pet store and bought a giant **steel cage**. They came in all different sizes for all different size dogs. When I described Marley to the clerk, he led us to the largest one of all. It was enormous and made out of heavy steel with two locks to hold the door securely shut. It was big enough for a lion to stand up and turn around in and had a heavy steel **pan** for a floor. This was our answer, our own portable prison.

Conor and Patrick both crawled inside and I slid the bolts shut, locking them in for a moment. "What do you guys think?" I asked. "Will this hold our super dog?"

Conor **teeter**ed at the cage door, his fingers through the bars, and said, "Me in jail."

"Waddy's going to be our prisoner!" Patrick chimed in, delighted **at the prospect**.

Back home, we set up the **crate** next to the washing machine. The cage **took up** nearly half the laundry room. "Come here, Marley!" I called when it was fully **assemble**d. I tossed a Milk-Bone in and he happily pranced in after it. I closed and **bolted the door** behind him, and he stood there chewing his **treat, unfazed** by

---

steel cage 강철 우리 pan 금속제 용기 teeter 비틀거리다 at the prospect 그 장면을 상상하면서 crate 골격을 갖춘 대형상자 take up (공간을) 차지하다 assemble 조립하다, 설치하다 bolt the door 빗장을 지르다, 걸쇠를 걸어잠그다 treat 선물, 접대 unfazed 동요(당황)하지 않는

the new life experience he was about to enter, the one known in prison as "solitary **confinement**."

"This is going to be your new home when we're away," I said cheerfully. Marley stood there panting contentedly, not a trace of concern on his face, and then he lay down and let out a sigh. "A good sign," I said to Jenny. "A very good sign."

That evening we decided to **give** the **maximum-security** dog jail cell **a test run**. This time I didn't even need a Milk-Bone to lure Marley in. I simply opened the gate, gave a whistle, and in he walked, tail banging the metal sides.

"Be a good boy, Marley," I said.

"You know something?" Jenny said as we loaded the boys in the minivan to go out to dinner.

"What?" I asked.

"This is the first time since we got him that I don't **have a knot in my stomach** leaving Marley alone in the house," she said. "I never even realized how much it put me **on edge** until now."

"I know what you mean," I said. "It was always a guessing game: 'What will our dog destroy this time?'"

---

confinement 감금   maximum-security 가장 안전한 상태의   give a test run 시운전하다, 시험해보다
have a knot in the stomach 불안하다, 조마조마하다   on edge 초조한, 조마조마한

"I think that crate is going to be the best money we ever spent," she said.

"We should have done this a long time ago," I agreed. "You can't put a price on peace of mind."

We had a great dinner out, followed by a sunset **stroll** on the beach. The boys **splash**ed in the **surf**, chased seagulls, and threw **fistful**s of sand in the water.

"What a nice outing this has been," Jenny said as we walked up the front sidewalk to our house.

I was about to agree with her when I noticed something out of the corner of my eye—something up ahead that was not quite right. I turned my head and stared at the window beside the front door. The miniblinds were shut, as they always were when we left the house. But about a foot up from the bottom of the window, the metal **slat**s were bent apart and something was sticking through them.

Something black. And wet. And pressed up against the glass.

"What the . . . ?" I said. "How could . . . ? Marley?"

When I opened the front door, sure enough, there was our one-dog welcoming committee, wiggling all over the foyer, **pleased as punch** to have us home again.

---

stroll 산책 splash 철벅철벅 소리를 내다. 물을 튀기다 surf 밀려드는 파도 fistful 한 움큼 slat 널조각
pleased as punch 의기양양한, 신이 난

We checked every room and closet for signs of Marley's unsupervised adventure. Amazingly, the house was fine. We **converged on** the laundry room. The crate's door stood wide open. It was as if some secret **accomplice** had **snuck in** and **sprung** our **inmate**.

I squatted down beside the cage to have a closer look. The two locks were both slid back in the open position, and they **were dripping with** saliva.

"It looks like an **inside job**," I said. "Somehow **Houdini** here licked his way out."

"I can't believe it," Jenny said.

We always **fancied** Marley to be as dumb as **alga**e, but he had been clever enough to figure out how to stick his long, strong tongue through the bars to slowly work the **barrel**s free from their **slot**s. He had **lick**ed his way to freedom. He proved over the coming weeks that he was able to easily repeat the trick whenever he wanted. Some days we would return to find him resting peacefully in the cage, other days to find him waiting at the front window.

We **took to wiring** both locks in place with heavy electrical cable. That worked for a while. But one day, with distant thunder **rumbling** on the horizon, we came

converge on 한 곳으로 모이다 accomplice 공범, 한패 sneak in 숨어들다, 잠입하다 spring 탈옥시 키다, 풀어주다 inmate 수감자 be dripping with 흠뻑 젖다, 잔뜩 묻어 있다 inside job 내부자 소행 Houdini 탈출 묘기로 유명한 마술사 후디니 fancy 추측하다, 여기다 alga 조류(藻類) barrel 걸쇠, 빗장 slot 홈, 가늘고 긴 구멍 lick 핥다 take to doing ~하는 것이 습관이 되다 rumble 우르릉거리다

home to find the bottom corner of the cage's gate had been peeled back. It looked as though someone had used a giant can opener. **Panicky** Marley was firmly stuck around the rib cage, half in and half out of the tight opening. I bent the steel gate back in place as best I could, and we began wiring all four corners of the door, as well as the locks. Pretty soon we were reinforcing the corners of the cage itself as Marley continued to put his **brawn** into **busting out**.

Within three months, the **gleam**ing steel cage we had thought was Marley-proof looked like it had taken a direct hit from a cannon. The bars were twisted and bent and the frame **pried apart**. The door hardly fit anymore, and the sides bulged outward. I continued to **reinforce** it as best I could, and it continued to hold **tenuously** against Marley's **full-bodied assault**s. Whatever false sense of security the **contraption** had once offered us was gone. Each time we left, even for a half hour, we wondered whether this would be the time that our **manic** inmate would bust out. When would he go on another couch-shredding, wall-gouging, door-eating **rampage**?

So much for peace of mind.

---

panicky 공포에 휩싸인 brawn 체력, 근육의 힘 bust out 탈출하다 gleam 빛나다 pry apart 사이를 벌리다 reinforce 보강하다 tenuously 취약하게 full-bodied 전면적인, 온몸의 assault 공격 contraption 장치 manic 미친, 제정신이 아닌 rampage 발작, 난리 법석 so much for (~은) 그것으로 끝, (~이여) 안녕

Reading Comprehension

1. What did Marley like best about the new house?

a. The house was in a better neighborhood in Boca Raton.
b. He got to sleep in the laundry instead of the garage.
c. There was a swimming pool.
d. There was a view of children's playground to watch.

2. Which of these reasons was not why the Grogans bought a cage for Marley?

a. to keep him safe
b. to stop him from destroying things while they were gone
c. to keep him secure during storms
d. to lock the children away from Marley

3. How did Marley escape from the cage?

a. He dug a hole under the cage.
b. He kept a secret key hidden in his mouth.
c. He slid the bolts across using his tongue.
d. He pushed the bars open using his head.

4. The following describes the cage after 3 months. Fill in the blanks with the correct words.

a. bulged   b. frame   c. bars   d. door

The _____ were twisted and bent and the _____ pried apart.
The _____ hardly fit anymore, and the sides _____ outward.

Answers: **1.** c   **2.** d   **3.** c   **4.** c-b-d-a

13

Dinner Time!

In **fancy-pants** Boca Raton, Marley **stuck out** like a sumo wrestler at a ballet. Boca had lots of small, **yappy**, **pampered** dogs. They were **precious** little things, often with **bow**s in their fur and **cologne spritz**ed on their necks. Some even had painted toenails. You would spot them in the most unlikely places — peeking out of a purse at you as you waited in line at the bagel shop or **snoozing** on towels at the beach. Mostly you could find them **cruising** around town in very expensive cars, sitting behind the steering wheels on their owners' laps. They were **petite** and

---

fancy-pants 세련된, (지나치게) 화려한, 속물적인 stick out 두드러지다, 눈에 띄다 yappy 말이 많은, (개가) 잘 짖는 pampered 사랑을 듬뿍 받는, 귀염둥이인 precious 사랑받는 bow 나비 리본 cologne 연한 향수 spritz 뿌리다 snooze 졸다, 낮잠을 자다 cruise 유유히 돌아다니다, 유람하다 petite 몸집이 작은, 왜소한

sophisticated. Marley was big and **clunky**. He *really* wanted to **hang out** with the popular **pooch**es. They wanted nothing to do with him.

Thanks to obedience school, Marley was fairly manageable on walks. But if he saw something he liked, he still wouldn't hesitate to lunge for it. He didn't care if he choked himself in the process.

Each time he spotted one of the pampered **pup**s around town, he would break into a gallop, **drag**ging Jenny or me behind him at the end of the leash. The choker chain would tighten around his throat, making him gasp and cough. Each time Marley would be **snub**bed—not only by the Boca minidog but by the Boca minidog's owner, *too*. The owner would snatch up young Fifi or Suzi or Cheri as if rescuing her from the jaws of an **alligator**. Marley did not seem to mind. When the next minidog came into sight, he would do it all over again.

One Sunday afternoon, Jenny and I thought it would be fun to take the whole family for an outside meal at one of the popular restaurants. We loaded the boys into the minivan. Even Marley came. In Boca, it was a tradition

---

sophisticated 세련된, 교양 있는   clunky 투박한, 촌스러운   hang out 함께 어울리다, 놀다   pooch 개
pup 강아지   drag 힘들여 끌다   snub 박대하다, 푸대접하다   alligator 악어

for dogs to eat at their owners' feet.

We found a restaurant with outside tables, and I hooked the end of Marley's leash to one of the legs. We ordered drinks all around.

"To a beautiful day with my beautiful family," Jenny said, holding up her glass for a toast. We clicked our glasses, and the boys smashed their **sippy cup**s into each other.

That's when it happened. It happened so fast, in fact, that we didn't even realize it had happened. All we knew was that our table started moving. It was **crash**ing its way through the sea of other tables.

Banging into innocent **bystander**s and making a horrible, **ear-piercing, industrial-grade shriek**, it scraped over the concrete sidewalk. What was going on? Was our table **under a spell**? I quickly saw that it wasn't our table that was **haunted**, but our dog. Marley was out in front, **chug**ging forward with every ounce of **rippling** muscle he had.

In the fraction of a second after that, I saw just where Marley was heading. Fifty feet down the sidewalk, a delicate French poodle **linger**ed at her owner's side, nose

---

sippy cup 유아용 컵   crash 요란한 소리를 내며 나아가다   bang 쿵 소리를 내며 충돌하다, 부딪히다
bystander 구경꾼   ear-piercing 귀청이 찢어질 것 같은   industrial-grade 산업 현장에서나 있을 법한
shriek 높고 날카로운 소리   under a spell 주문/마법에 걸린   haunted 귀신들린   chug 헉헉대며 나아가다
rippling 울룩불룩한   linger 계속 머무르다

in the air.

Jenny and I both sat there for a moment longer, drinks in hand, the boys between us in their stroller. We wanted our perfect little Sunday afternoon to last. There was just one problem—our table was now **motor**ing its way through the crowd. An instant later, we were on our feet, screaming and running.

"Sorry!" we said to the customers around us. "Really really sorry."

I was the first to reach the runaway table. I grabbed on, **planted my feet**, and leaned back with everything I had. Soon Jenny was beside me, pulling back too. I felt like we were action heroes in a Western movie, giving our all to rein in the runaway train before it jumped the tracks and **plunge**d over a cliff.

When we finally got the table stopped and Marley reeled in, just feet from the poodle and her mortified owner, I turned back to check on the boys. That's when I **got** my first **good look at** the faces of my fellow diners. Men stopped **in midconversation**, cell phones in their hands. Women stared with opened mouths.

It was finally Conor who broke the silence. "Waddy go

---

motor 달려가다　plant one's feet 발을 땅에 힘껏 붙이고 버티다　plunge 추락하다, 몸을 던지다　get a good look at (~을) 똑똑히 보다　in midconversation 한창 이야기하는 중에

walk!" he screamed with delight.

A waiter rushed up and helped me drag the table back into place as Jenny held Marley **in a death grip**. He still hadn't taken his eyes off the poodle. "Let me get some new place settings," the waiter said.

"That won't be necessary," Jenny said **nonchalantly**. "We'll just pay for our drinks and go."

Soon after our outdoor dining **fiasco**, I found a book in the library titled *No Bad Dogs* by Barbara Woodhouse. The author believed that if a dog **misbehave**d, it wasn't the dog's problem. It was a problem with the people who hadn't trained him very well. The book described some of the worst **canine** behaviors imaginable.

There were dogs that **howl**ed **nonstop**, dug nonstop, fought nonstop, and bit nonstop. There were dogs that hated all men and dogs that hated all women. Dogs that stole from their masters and dogs that jealously attacked **defenseless** infants. There were even dogs that ate their own poop. *Thank God,* I thought, *at least he doesn't eat his own poop.*

in a death grip (행여 놓칠세라) 단단히 부여잡고   nonchalantly 아무렇지 않게   fiasco 대실패, 대망신
misbehave 못된 짓을 하다, 버릇없이 굴다   canine 개의   howl 늑대 울음소리를 내다   nonstop 쉬지 않고
defenseless 무방비 상태인, 방어 능력이 없는

Not long after I read Woodhouse's book, a neighbor asked us to **take in** their cat for a week while they were on vacation.

"Sure," we said. "Bring him over." Compared to a dog, cats were easy. Cats **ran on autopilot**. This cat was shy and **elusive**, especially around Marley. He hid under the couch all day and came out to eat his food and use the **kitty litter box** when we were asleep. We kept the food high out of Marley's reach and **tucked** the litter box **away** in a corner of the patio. There was nothing to it, really. Marley was totally unaware the cat was even in the house.

Midway through the cat's stay with us, I awoke at dawn to a loud, **driving beat** traveling through the mattress. It was Marley, quivering with excitement beside the bed, his tail slapping the mattress at a furious rate. *Whomp! Whomp! Whomp!* I reached out to pet him. He began prancing and dancing beside the bed. The Marley Mambo.

"Okay, what do you have?" I asked him, eyes still shut. As if to answer, Marley proudly plopped his prize onto the **crisp** sheets, just inches from my face. In my **groggy**

---

take in 잠시 맡아 돌보아주다　run on autopilot 행동이 일정한 패턴을 따르다　elusive 잘 잡히지 않는, 요
리조리 빠져나가는　kitty 새끼 고양이, 고양이를 귀엽게 이르는 말　litter box 고양이 배변 상자　tuck away
(안전한 곳에) 치우다, 감추다　midway 중간쯤에　driving 격렬한, 드센　beat 두드리는 소리　crisp 깨끗한, 단
정한　groggy 몸을 가누지 못하는, 정신이 혼미한

state, it took me a minute to process what exactly it was. The object was small, dark, and coated in a **coarse**, **gritty** sand. Then the smell reached my nostrils. An **acrid**, **pungent**, **putrid** smell. I **bolted upright** and pushed backward against Jenny, waking her up. I pointed at Marley's gift to us, **glisten**ing on the sheets.

"That's not . . . ," Jenny began, disgust in her voice.

"Yes, it is," I said. "He raided the kitty litter box."

Marley could not have looked more pleased had he just presented us with the **Hope Diamond**. As Barbara Woodhouse had predicted, our mentally unstable, abnormal mutt had entered the poop-eating stage of his life.

---

coarse 거친 gritty 자갈이 섞인, 모래투성이의 acrid 매운, 매캐한 pungent 톡 쏘는 putrid 썩는 냄새가 나는 bolt upright 똑바로 일어나 앉다 glisten 빛나다, 반짝이다 Hope Diamond 세계 최대의 블루 다이아몬드

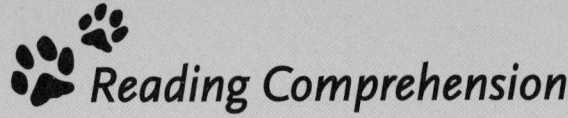
Reading Comprehension

1. Which best describes how other dog owners felt about Marley?

a. friendly and welcoming
b. defensive and overprotective
c. cold and indifferent
d. excited and enthusiastic

2. What is the tradition in Boca Raton?

a. to drive your dog around town
b. to make sure your dog gets bows in their hair
c. to run after the other dogs to greet them
d. to have your dog sit under the table at outdoor restaurants

3. Place the following scenes in order.

a. Jenny and John are apologizing as they run after Marley.
b. The family is toasting their drinks while sitting at the table.
c. Marley is running, and dragging the table off down the street.
d. They are paying for their drinks and leaving.

4. Match the following to their hiding place where they belong.

a. cat   1) kitty litter box
b. cat food   2) high on a shelf
c. poop   3) in the corner of the patio
d. kitty litter box   4) under the sofa

Answers: **1.** b **2.** d **3.** b-c-a-d **4.** a-4, b-2, c-1, d-3

14

Lightning Strikes

 On January 9, 1997, Jenny gave me a **belated** Christmas present: a pink-cheeked, seven-pound baby girl. We named her Colleen.

When Colleen was one week old, Jenny brought her outside for the first time. The day was **crisp** and beautiful, and the boys and I were in the front yard, planting flowers. Marley was chained to a tree nearby, happy to lie in the shade and watch the world go by.

Jenny sat in the grass beside Marley and put Colleen in a portable **bassinette** on the ground between them. After several minutes, the boys called for Mom to come

belated 때늦은 crisp 서늘하고 상쾌한, 청량한 bassinette 요람

closer to see what they had planted. They led Jenny and me around the garden beds as Colleen napped in the shade beside Marley. We wandered behind some large **shrubbery**. We could still see the baby, but from the street no one could see us.

An older couple walking by had stopped and were gawking at the scene in our front yard with bewildered expressions. We peeked at them through the shrubs. At first I was not sure what had made them stop and stare. Then it hit me: All they could see was a **fragile** newborn alone with a large yellow dog, who appeared to be babysitting **single-handedly**. They had no idea we were right there.

There was Marley, looking like an Egyptian sphinx, lying with his front paws crossed, head up, panting contentedly. Every few seconds he sniffed the baby's head. Then Marley rested his chin across the baby's stomach, his head bigger than her whole body, and let out a long sigh. It was as if he were saying, "When are those two going to get home?" It looked like he was protecting her, and maybe he was, but I'm pretty sure he was just trying to get a whiff of her **diaper**.

---

shrubbery 관목 숲 fragile 연약한 single-handedly 혼자, 홀로 diaper 기저귀

Jenny and I stood there in the bushes and exchanged grins. The thought of Marley as doggie day care was just too good to let go. I **was tempted to wait** there and see how the scene would play out, but I was afraid the couple might call 911. We stepped out of the bushes and waved to the couple, who looked relieved to see us.

"You must really trust your dog," the woman said.

"He hasn't eaten one yet," I said.

When Marley was about six years old, his intense fear of thunder finally made sense. I was in the backyard on a Sunday afternoon. The skies grew darker as I dug up **a rectangle of** grass to plant a vegetable garden. Marley paced nervously around me. His internal **barometer** told him a storm was coming. I sensed it, too, but I wanted to get the project done. I figured I would work until I felt the first drops of rain. As I dug, I kept glancing at the sky, watching an **ominous** black thunderhead far away, out over the ocean. Marley was whining softly, **beckon**ing me to put down the shovel and head inside.

"Relax," I told him. "It's still miles away."

The words had barely left my lips when I felt a kind of

---

be tempted to do (~을) 하고 싶은 마음이 들다 a rectangle of 직사각형 모양의 barometer 바로미터, 잣대, 기압계 ominous 음산한, 위협적인, 불길한 beckon 유인하다, (~을) 하게 하다

quivering **tingle** on the back of my neck. The sky had turned an odd shade of olive-gray. The air went **dead** as though some heavenly force had grabbed the winds and frozen them in its **grip**.

Weird, I thought as I leaned on my shovel to study the sky. That's when I heard it—a **buzzing**, **popping**, **crackling surge** of energy. *Pffffffffffft.* The sound filled the air around me. Then silence. I knew trouble was coming, but I had no time to react. In the next fraction of a second, the sky went pure, blindingly white. An explosion **boom**ed in my ears. I had never heard anything like it before—not in any storm, at any fireworks display, or at any **demolition site**. A wall of energy hit me in the chest like an invisible linebacker.

I don't know how many seconds later I opened my eyes. I was lying facedown on the ground with sand in my mouth. Marley was down, too—**in his hit-the-deck stance**. When he saw me raise my head, he wiggled toward me on his belly like a soldier trying to slide beneath **barbed wire**. Reaching me, he climbed right on my back and buried his snout in my neck, frantically licking me.

---

tingle 저릿함, 오싹함　dead 매우 고요한, 정적이 맴도는　grip 움켜쥔 손아귀　buzzing 우르릉　popping 쾅　crackling 쫘직, 우지직　surge 쇄도, 돌진　boom (소리가) 울려 퍼지다　demolition site 철거 현장　in a stance (~한) 자세로　hit the deck 바닥에 납작 엎드리다　barbed wire 가시 철조망

"Come on!" I yelled. Marley and I were on our feet, sprinting through the **downpour** toward the back door as new bolts of lightning flashed around us. We did not stop until we were safely inside. I knelt on the floor, soaking wet, catching my breath. Marley **clambered** all **over** me, licking my face, nibbling my ears, **fling**ing spit and loose fur all over everything. He was beside himself with fear, shaking uncontrollably, **drool** hanging off his chin. I hugged him and tried to calm him down.

"**That was close**!" I said, and realized that I was shaking, too.

Marley looked up at me with those big eyes that I swore could almost talk. I was sure I knew what he was trying to tell me. "I've been trying to warn you for years that this stuff can kill you. But would anyone listen? Now will you take me seriously?"

The dog had a point.

Maybe his fear of thunder had not been so crazy after all. I pulled Marley into my lap, all ninety-seven nervous pounds of him, and made him a promise right then and there: Never again would I **dismiss** his fear of this deadly force of nature.

---

downpour 폭우, 억수같이 쏟아지는 비　clamber over 기어서 올라가다　fling 흩뿌리다, 튀기다　drool 침
that was close 아슬아슬했어, 큰일 날 뻔했어.　dismiss 무시하다, (근심 걱정 따위를) 쫓아내다

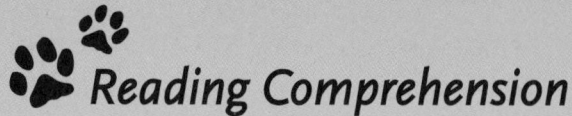
Reading Comprehension

1. What Christmas present did Jenny give John?

a. a new dog   b. a baby girl
c. a new house   d. a baby boy

2. Choose the correct word.

There was Marley, looking like an Egyptian (sphinx/lion).
Every few seconds, he (licked/sniffed) the baby's head.
Then Marley rested his (chin/paws) across the baby's stomach.
He let out a long (roar/sigh).

3. Which of these best describes how John and Marley felt during the storm?

a. surprised and excited
b. stunned and scared
c. shocked and angry
d. dazed and upset

4. What did John learn from his experience of the storm?

a. Marley is right to fear the storms.
b. Florida is a bad place to live.
c. He should not garden in bad weather.
d. It is dangerous to plant vegetables.

Answers: **1.** b **2.** sphinx, sniffed, chin, sigh **3.** b **4.** a

15

Dog Beach

On a **drop-dead**-perfect June morning, Marley and I headed for Dog Beach.

Dog Beach was one of the last stretches of ocean sand in Florida where dogs and their owners could play. The rules were simple: **Aggressive** dogs had to stay leashed. All others could run free. Owners were to bring plastic bags with them to pick up any poop. All trash, including **bag**ged dog waste, was to be **carted out**. Each dog was supposed to arrive with a supply of fresh drinking water.

But the most important rule: No pooping in the water.

drop-dead 넋이 나갈 정도로, 굉장히 aggressive 공격적인 bag 봉지에 담다 cart out 치우다, 없애다

I filled the car with as many beach towels as I could find—and that was just for the drive over. As always, Marley's tongue was hanging out, spit flying everywhere. I felt like I was on a road trip with **Old Faithful**. My only regret was that the windshield wipers were not on the inside.

I parked the car and began the long hike to the beach. Marley **led the charge**. Just as we reached the path to the water, Marley squatted in the weeds and laid a giant **log**. Perfect. At least that was **out of the way**. I bagged it up.

"To the beach!" I commanded.

As we came up over the top of the sand **dune**, I was surprised to see several people **wading** in the shallow water with their dogs on leashes. I expected the dogs to be **romp**ing and playing together off their leashes.

"What's going on?" I wondered out loud.

"A **sheriff's deputy** was just here," one **glum** dog owner explained to me. "He said from now on they're **enforcing** the county **leash law**. We'll be **fine**d if our dogs are **loose**."

I was too late. The police were tightening the **noose**. I

Old Faithful 옐로스톤 국립공원의 간헐천　lead the charge 앞장서서 공격에 나서다　log 장작　out of the way 끝낸, 해결이 된　dune 모래 언덕　wade 헤치며 걷다　romp 즐겁게 뛰놀다　sheriff's deputy 부보안관　glum 침울한, 시무룩한　enforce (법을) 집행하다　leash law 견주의 소유지 밖에서는 개에게 목줄을 채워야 한다는 법령　fine (~에게) 벌금을 부과하다　loose 풀린, 묶여 있지 않은　noose 올가미

obediently walked Marley along the water's edge with the other dog owners. It felt more like prison than paradise.

I returned with Marley to my towel and poured him a bowl of water from the **canteen**. A shirtless, tattooed man in **cutoff blue jeans** and work boots came over the dune leading a muscular and **fierce-looking** pit bull terrier on a heavy chain.

The owner must have seen my fear. "Don't you worry," he called out. "Killer's friendly. He don't never fight other dogs." I was just beginning to **exhale with relief** when he added, "But you should see him rip open a **wild hog**! I'll tell you, he can get it down and **gut**ted in about fifteen seconds."

Marley and Killer the Pig-**Slay**ing Pit Bull strained at their leashes, circling, sniffing furiously at each other. Marley had never been in a fight in his life. He was so much bigger than most other dogs that he had never been intimidated by a challenge, either. Even when a dog attempted to **pick a fight**, he didn't take the hint. He would pounce into a playful stance, butt up, tail wagging, a **dumb**, happy grin on his face. But he had never before **been confronted by** a trained killer. I pictured Killer

---

canteen 물통, 매점 cutoff blue jeans 청바지의 무릎 아래 부위를 잘라낸 반바지 fierce 사나운, 험악한 -looking ~하게 생긴, ~한 외모의 exhale with relief 안도의 한숨을 내쉬다 wild hog 멧돼지 gut 배를 갈라 내장을 발라내다, 찢어발기다 slay 난도질하다 pick a fight 싸움을 걸다, 도발하다 dumb 멍청한, 우둔한 be confronted by (곤란이나 힘든 상황과) 맞닥뜨리다, 대면하다

lunging without warning for Marley's throat and not letting go.

But Killer's owner wasn't concerned. "Unless you're a wild hog, he'll just lick you to death," he said.

I told him the cops had just been here and were going to **ticket** people who did not obey the leash law. "I guess they're **cracking down**," I said.

The man yelled and spit into the sand. "I've been bringing my dogs to this beach for years. You don't need no leash at Dog Beach!" He unclipped the heavy chain, and Killer galloped across the sand and into the water. Marley reared back on his hind legs, bouncing up and down. He looked at Killer and then up at me. He looked back at Killer and back at me. His paws **pad**ded nervously on the sand and he let out a soft whimper. I looked around. No police were anywhere in sight. I looked at Marley. If he could talk, I knew he would say, "Please! Please! Pretty please! I'll be good. I promise."

"Go ahead, let him loose," Killer's owner said. "A dog ain't meant to spend his life on the end of a rope."

"Oh, what the heck," I said, and unsnapped the leash. Marley dashed for the water, kicking sand all over us as

ticket (벌금을 부과하는) 위반딱지를 떼다   crack down 엄중 단속하다   pad 살금살금 걷다

he blasted off. He crashed into the surf just as a **breaker** rolled in, **toss**ing him under water. A second later his head reappeared. The instant he got back on his feet, he threw a cross-body block at Killer the Pig-Slaying Pit Bull. They both went down into water. Together they rolled beneath a wave. When they popped back up again, their tails were wagging, their mouths grinning. Killer jumped on Marley's back and Marley on Killer's, their jaws **clamp**ing playfully around each other's throats. They chased each other up the waterline and back again, sending plumes of spray flying on either side of them. They pranced, they danced, they wrestled, they dove. I don't think I had ever before, or have ever since seen such pure joy.

Pretty soon all the dogs on the beach were running free. The twelve or so dogs all got along incredibly well. The owners all followed the rules. It was Dog Beach as it was meant to be.

There was only one small problem. As the morning went on, Marley kept **lap**ping up saltwater. I followed behind him with the bowl of fresh water, but he was too distracted to drink. Several times I led him right up to the

---

breaker 해안에 밀려와 부서지는 큰 파도 **toss** 내던지다 **clamp** 꽉 조이다, 물다 **lap** 핥아먹다, 마시다

bowl and stuck his nose into it, but he rejected the fresh water as if it were **vinegar**.

Out in the shallow water, he paused from his play to lap up even more saltwater. "Stop that, you **dummy**," I yelled at him. "You're going to make yourself—"

Before I could finish my thought, it happened. A strange **glaze** settled over his eyes. A horrible churning sound began to **erupt** from his gut. He arched his back high and opened and shut his mouth several times, as if trying to clear something from his craw. His shoulders heaved. His **abdomen contort**ed.

I hurried to finish my sentence. "—sick."

The same instant that word left my lips, Marley committed the ultimate Dog Beach **no-no**.

"*GAAAAAAAAACK!*" Marley let out the sound in that moment.

I raced to pull him out of the water, but it was too late. Everything was coming up.

"*GAAAAAAAAACK!*" I could see last night's dog chow floating on the water's surface. I could see undigested **corn kernel**s that he had **swipe**d off the kids' plates **bob**bing among the **nugget**s. A milk-**jug**

---

vinegar 식초 dummy 멍청이, 바보 glaze (눈빛이) 멍함, 게슴츠레함, 번뜩거림 erupt 분출하다
abdomen 배, 복부 contort 꿈틀거리다, 뒤틀리다 no-no 금지된 것/행동 corn kernel 옥수수 알갱이
swipe 훔쳐 먹다 bob (물 위에) 둥둥 떠다니다 nugget 작은 덩어리 jug 병

cap and the **sever**ed head of a tiny plastic soldier also appeared.

The whole embarrassing episode took fewer than three seconds. The instant his stomach was emptied, he looked up brightly, as if to say, "Now that I've got that taken care of, who wants to body surf?"

I glanced nervously around me, but no one had seemed to notice. The other dog owners were occupied with their own dogs, farther down the beach. Nearby, a mother helped her toddler make a sand castle. The sunbathers were lying flat on their backs, eyes closed.

Thank goodness! I thought. I waded into Marley's **puke** zone, stirring the water with my feet to hide the evidence. *How embarrassing would that have been?* Maybe we had broken the No. 1 Dog Beach Rule, but we hadn't caused any real harm. After all, it was just undigested food. The fish would be thankful for the meal. Wouldn't they? I even picked out the milk-jug cap and soldier's head and put them in my pocket. I didn't want to litter.

"Listen you," I said sternly, grabbing Marley around the snout and forcing him to look me in the eye. "Stop

sever 완전히 잘라내다　puke 토사물

drinking saltwater. What kind of a dog doesn't know enough to not drink saltwater?" I thought about **yank**ing him off the beach and cutting our adventure short, but now he seemed fine. There couldn't possibly be anything left in his stomach. The damage was done, and we had gotten away with it. I released him, and he streaked down the beach to play with Killer.

But there was something I hadn't thought of. Marley's stomach may have been completely **emptied**, but his **bowel**s were not. The sun was reflecting blindingly off the water. I **squint**ed to see Marley **frolic**king among the other dogs. As I watched, he stopped playing and began turning in tight circles in the shallow water. I knew what that meant. It was what he did every morning in the backyard after breakfast. Sometimes the circling could go on for a minute or more as he sought just the perfect patch of earth on which to relieve himself. And now he was circling in the shallows of Dog Beach—where no dog had dared to poop before. *Oh, no!*

When he finished circling, Marley squatted. And this time, he had an audience. Killer's dad and several other dog owners were standing just a few yards from him.

---

yank 잡아당기다, 끌어내다   empty 뱃속을 비우다   bowel 장(腸), 창자   squint 눈을 가늘게 뜨고 보다
frolic 즐겁게/해맑게 뛰어놀다

The mother and her daughter had turned from their sand castle to gaze out to sea. A couple holding hands walked along the water's edge.

"No," I whispered to Marley—even though he couldn't hear. "Please, no."

"Hey!" someone yelled out. "**Get** your dog!"

"Stop him!" someone else shouted.

As alarmed voices cried out, the sunbathers sat up to see what all the **commotion** was about.

I **burst into** a full sprint. I had to get to him before it was too late. If I could just reach him and yank him out of his squat before he let loose, I might be able to stop him. Each step seemed to last forever. Each foot hit the sand with a dull thud. My arms swung through the air. My face **scrunch**ed in a sort of agonized grimace.

I felt as if I was moving in slow motion. So was everything around me. A young woman sunbather plastered her hand over her mouth. The mother scooped up her child and retreated from the water's edge. The dog owners, their faces twisted with disgust, pointed. Killer's dad, his **leathery** neck bulging, yelled. Marley was done circling now and in full squat position, looking up to the

get 데려가다 commotion 소란, 소동 burst into 갑자기 ~하기 시작하다 scrunch 일그러지다
leathery 가죽처럼 질기고 유연한

heavens as if saying a little prayer.

"Nooooooooooooooooo!" I screamed. I was almost there, just feet from him. "Marley, no! No, Marley, No! No! No! No!" It was no use. Just as I reached him, he exploded in a burst of watery **diarrhea**. Everyone was jumping back now, fleeing to higher ground. Owners grabbed their dogs. Sunbathers scooped up their towels.

Then it was over. Marley trotted out of the water onto the beach, shook off, and turned to look at me, panting happily. I pulled a plastic bag out of my pocket and held it helplessly in the air. It was useless. The waves crashed in and spread Marley's mess across the water and up onto the beach.

"Dude," Killer's dad said. "That was not cool."

No, it wasn't cool at all. Marley and I had violated the most important rule of Dog Beach. We had vomited and pooped in the water—and ruined the morning for everyone. It was time to leave. Quickly.

"Sorry," I mumbled to Killer's owner as I snapped the leash on Marley. "He swallowed a bunch of seawater."

Back at the car, I threw a towel over Marley and vigorously rubbed him down. The more I rubbed, the

diarrhea 설사

more he shook. Soon I was covered in sand and spray and fur. I wanted to be mad at him. I wanted to strangle him.

But it was too late now. Besides, Marley hadn't meant to do it. He hadn't disobeyed a command or purposely tried to humiliate me. He simply had to go, and he went. It just happened to be at the wrong place and wrong time and in front of all the wrong people. I could have killed him, except I knew he was a victim of his own tiny brain. He was the only beast on the whole beach dumb enough to **guzzle** seawater. How could I hold that against him?

"You don't have to look so pleased with yourself," I said as I loaded him into the backseat. But pleased he was. He could not have looked happier had I bought him his own Caribbean island. What he did not know was that this would be his last time setting a paw in any body of saltwater. His days as a **beach bum** were over.

guzzle 마구 마셔대다. 먹어대다   beach bum 해변에서 빈둥거리는 사람

Reading Comprehension

1. Which of these is not a rule for Dog Beach?

a. Always bring a plastic bag to pick up your dog's poop.
b. Always bring fresh water for your dog to drink.
c. Never let your dog poop in the water.
d. Aggressive dogs can run without a leash.

2. Why did Marley get sick at the beach?

a. He kept drinking saltwater.
b. He ate sand.
c. He got sea sick.
d. He had eaten too much before he arrived.

3. Choose the correct word.

Marley was (frolicking/attacking) the other dogs.
He stopped playing and started (drinking/circling) in the water.
I knew what that meant because he did it every (morning/afternoon).
Marley was about to (poop/swim) in the water.

4. How did John feel about Marley pooping in the water?

a. angry and upset
b. disgusted and angry
c. proud and pleased
d. appalled and humiliated

Answers: **1.** d **2.** a **3.** frolicking, circling, morning, poop **4.** d

16

A Northbound Plane

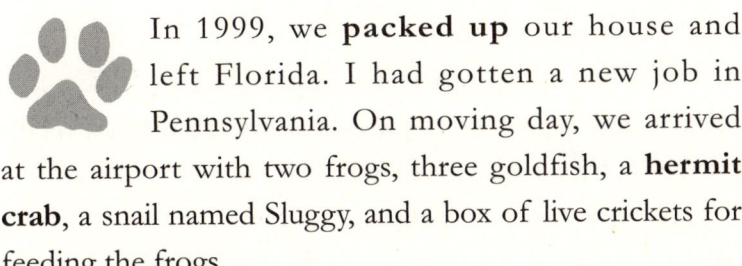
In 1999, we **packed up** our house and left Florida. I had gotten a new job in Pennsylvania. On moving day, we arrived at the airport with two frogs, three goldfish, a **hermit crab**, a snail named Sluggy, and a box of live crickets for feeding the frogs.

And, of course, Marley. Like most things that involved Marley, getting him on the plane wasn't easy. He had to ride in a crate where the luggage was stored.

We stepped up to the airline counter with Marley on his leash. A woman in uniform looked at Marley, then looked

pack up 정리하다, 팔다 hermit crab 소라게

at the crate I had brought for him. "We can't allow that dog **aboard** in that container," she said. "He's too big for it."

"The pet store said this was the 'large dog' size," I pleaded. (I hadn't actually checked to make sure our *very* large dog would fit.)

"Airline rules say that the dog has to be able to stand up and turn all the way around," she explained. "Go ahead. Give it a try."

I opened the gate and called Marley. He **was not about to** voluntarily **walk** into jail. I pushed him and **prod**ded him. He didn't budge.

I searched my pockets for something to **bribe** him with. Where were the dog biscuits when I needed them? I found a **tin** of breath mints.

This is as good as it's going to get, I thought. I took one out and held it in front of his nose. "Want a mint, Marley? Go get the mint!" and I tossed it into the crate. Sure enough, he took the bait and walked right into the box.

The lady was right. He didn't quite fit. He **scrunched down** so his head wouldn't hit the ceiling. His **butt stuck**

---

aboard 탑승하는 be not about to do ~할 의사가 없다 prod 쿡쿡 찌르다 bribe 뇌물로 꼬드기다 tin 통, 깡통 scrunch down 쪼그려 앉다 butt 엉덩이 stick out 튀어나오다, 비어져 나오다

out the open door.

I scrunched his tail down and closed the gate, shoving his **rear** inside. "See?" I said. "He fits."

"He's got to be able to turn around," the woman told me.

"Turn around, boy," I called, giving a little whistle. "Come on, turn around."

Marley shot a glance at me over his shoulder. His eyes were asking, "And how do you expect me to do that?"

If Marley couldn't turn around, the airline was not letting him on the plane. I checked my watch. We had twelve minutes to **make the flight**.

"Come here, Marley!" I said more desperately. "Come on!" I snapped my fingers, rattled the metal gate, made **kissy-kissy** sounds. "Come on," I pleaded. "Turn around."

I **was about to drop** to my knees and beg when I heard a crash.

"Oops," Patrick said.

"The frogs are **loose**!" Jenny screamed, jumping into action.

"Froggy! Croaky! Come back!" the boys yelled **in unison**.

---

rear 궁둥이　**make a flight** 비행기를 타다, 비행을 하다　**kissy-kissy** 혀를 쭈쭈 차는 소리　**be about to do** 막 ~하려던 참이다　**loose** 풀려난　**in unison** 일제히, 동시에

Jenny was **on all fours** now, racing around the terminal. The frogs stayed one hop ahead of her. **Passersby** stopped and stared. From a distance you could not see the frogs at all, just the crazy lady with the diaper bag hanging from her neck. Looking at their faces, I could tell they fully expected her to start howling at any moment.

"Excuse me a second," I said as calmly as I could to the airline worker. Then I got down on my hands and knees, too.

Just as they were about to **leap out** the automatic doors, we captured Froggy and Croaky. As we turned back, I heard a **mighty ruckus** coming from the dog crate. The entire box shivered and lurched across the floor, and when I peered in I saw that Marley had somehow gotten himself turned around.

"See?" I said to the baggage supervisor. "He can turn around, no problem."

"Okay," she said **with a frown**. "But you're really pushing it."

Two workers lifted Marley and his crate onto a **dolly** and wheeled him away. The rest of us raced for our flight, arriving at the gate just as the flight attendants

---

on all fours 엉금엉금 기는   passerby 행인   leap out 튀어나가다   mighty 엄청난   ruckus 대소동   with a frown 인상을 쓰고   dolly 짐수레

were closing the **hatch**.

"Wait! We're here!" I shouted, pushing Colleen ahead of me. The boys and Jenny **trail**ed by fifty feet.

As we settled into our seats, I breathed a sigh of relief. We had gotten Marley **squared away**. We had recaptured the frogs. We had made the flight. Next stop, Allentown, Pennsylvania. I could relax now.

Through the window I watched as a **tram** pulled up with the dog crate sitting on it. "Look," I said to the kids. "There's Marley." They waved out the window and called, "Hi, Waddy."

As the engines **rev**ved, I pulled out a magazine. That's when I noticed Jenny freeze in the row in front of me. Then I heard it, too. From below our feet, deep in **the bowels of** the plane, came a muffled sound. Starting low and **mournful** it rose as it went. *Oh, dear!* I thought. *He's down there howling.*

Just so you know, Labrador retrievers do not howl. Beagles howl. Wolves howl. Labs do not howl, at least not well. Marley had attempted to howl twice before, both times in answer to a passing police siren, tossing back his head, forming his mouth into an *O* shape, and

---

hatch 출입문 trail 줄지어 뒤쫓아 오다 square away 성공적으로 처리하다 tram 짐차 rev 엔진의 가동 속도를 올리다 the bowels of ~의 깊숙한 내부 mournful 애절한, 구슬픈

letting loose the most pathetic sound I have ever heard, more like he was **gargling** than answering the call of the wild. But now, no question about it, he was howling.

The passengers began to look up from their newspapers and novels. A flight attendant handing out pillows paused and **cock**ed her head **quizzically**.

"Listen. Do you hear that?" a woman across the aisle asked her husband. "I think it's a dog." Jenny stared straight ahead. I stared into my magazine. If anyone asked, we were denying **ownership**.

"Waddy's sad," Patrick said.

I just pulled my magazine higher over my face. The jet engines whined and the plane **taxi**ed down the runway, **drowning out** Marley. I pictured him down below in the dark **hold**, alone, scared, confused, not even able to fully stand up. I imagined the roaring engines. To Marley, they probably sounded like another **thunderous** assault by random **lightning bolts** determined to **take him out**. The poor guy. I knew I would be spending the whole flight worrying about him.

The airplane was barely off the ground when I heard another little crash.

---

let loose (소리를) 내다　gargle 꼬르륵 소리를 내며 물로 입안을 헹구다　cock 고개를 갸우뚱하다, 들다　quizzically 이상하다는 듯이　ownership 소유권　taxi 비행기가 서서히 달리다　drown out 더 큰 소리로 (~의) 소리를 삼키다/뒤덮다　hold 화물실　thunderous 천둥이 치는 것처럼 매우 시끄러운　lightning bolts 번쩍하는 번갯불　take someone out 죽이다, 없애다

"Oops," Conor said.

I looked down and then stared straight into my magazine. After several seconds, I **glanced around**. When I was pretty sure no one was staring, I leaned forward and whispered into Jenny's ear, "Don't look now, but the crickets are loose."

glance around 휙 둘러보다

Reading Comprehension

1. Which is not a family pet of the Grogans?

a. Sluggy the snail
b. Marley the dog
c. Croaky the frog
d. Charlie the cat

2. Why was the airline worker reluctant to let Marley onto the plane?

a. He was poorly behaved.
b. His cage was too small.
c. They had too many pets.
d. Marley was too noisy with his howling.

3. Choose the correct word.

From below our (feet/seats), deep in the (bowels/stomach) of the plane, came a (clear/muffled) sound.
Oh dear! I thought. He's down there (crying/howling).

4. How did the author feel about Marley on the plane trip?

a. excited and happy
b. calm and relaxed
c. worried and sympathetic
d. embarrassed and uncomfortable

Answers: **1.** d **2.** b **3.** feet, bowels, muffled, howling **4.** c

17

In the Land of Pencils

In Pennsylvania we moved into a **rambling** house with a huge yard. Our property had woods and a **meadow** where we could pick wild raspberries. Marley and the kids loved getting **muddy** in the small **creek**.

There was only one thing missing. Minutes after we pulled into the driveway of our new house, Conor, who was five, looked up and declared, "I thought there were going to be pencils in Pencilvania." Big tears rolled from his eyes.

For our boys, now ages seven and five, this was a **near**

---

rambling (모양이) 불규칙한, 들쭉날쭉한 meadow 풀밭 muddy 진흙투성이가 된 creek 샛강, 개울, 시내
near 거의 ~이나 다름없는

deal breaker. Given the name of the state we were adopting, both of them arrived fully expecting to see bright yellow writing **implement**s hanging like berries from every tree and shrub, there for the **plucking**. They were **crushed** to learn otherwise.

Marley, on the other hand, had no problem with our home. He **fit** right **into** the new country lifestyle. He raced across the lawn and crashed through the **bramble**s. The neighborhood rabbits considered my garden their own personal salad bar. Marley made it his mission to catch one of the **diner**s. He would spot a rabbit **munch**ing the **lettuce** and barrel off down the hill **in hot pursuit**. His ears flapped behind him, his paws pounded the ground, and his bark filled the air. He was about as **sneaky** as a **marching band**. He never got closer than a dozen feet before his **intended** prey **scamper**ed off into the woods to safety. Five minutes later he'd do it all over again. Fortunately, he **was** no **better at sneaking up on** the skunks.

Autumn came and with it a whole new **mischievous** game—Attack the Leaf Pile. Trees did not **shed** their leaves in the fall in Florida. In Pennsylvania, Marley was

---

deal breaker 협상을 방해하는 요소 implement 도구, 기구 plucking 따기 crushed 상심한, 상처받은, 마음 아파하는 fit into (~에) 적응하다 bramble 검은딸기나무 diner 식사를 하는 사람 munch 우적우적 씹어먹다 lettuce 상추 in hot pursuit 열심히 뒤쫓아, 열띤 추격을 벌여 sneaky 은밀한, 교활한 marching band 군악대 intended 목표인, 목표로 삼은 scamper 날쌔게 움직이다, 재빨리 도망치다 be better at doing ~을 더 잘하다 sneak up on 살금살금 접근하다 mischievous 짓궂은 shed 뚝뚝 떨어뜨리다

positively convinced the falling leaves were a gift meant just for him.

As I **rake**d the orange and yellow leaves into giant heaps, Marley would sit and watch patiently, waiting until just the right moment to attack. After I had gathered a **towering** pile, he would **slink** forward, **crouch**ed low. Every few steps, he would stop, front paw raised, to sniff the air like a lion **stalk**ing an **unsuspecting gazelle**. Then, just as I raked the last leaf, he would lunge. Charging across the lawn in a series of bounding leaps, he would fly for the last several feet and land in a giant **belly flop** in the middle of the pile. He growled and rolled and flailed and **scratch**ed and **snap**ped and fiercely chased his tail, not stopping until my neat leaf pile was scattered across the lawn again. With the shredded remains of leaves **clinging to** his fur, he would sit up and give me a self-satisfied look, proud that he'd been such a big help.

Our first Christmas in Pennsylvania was supposed to be white. To convince Patrick and Conor to leave their home and friends in Florida, Jenny and I had promised them snow. As the holidays neared, the boys and Colleen

---

rake 갈퀴로 긁어모으다　towering 우뚝 솟은, 치솟은　slink 살금살금 움직이다　crouch 몸을 웅크리다　stalk 몰래 접근하다　unsuspecting 의심하지 않는　gazelle 가젤 (아프리카의 작은 영양)　belly flop 배치기 다이빙　scratch 긁다　snap 꽉 물다, 이빨을 딱딱 부딪히다　cling to (~에) 매달려/붙어 있다

sat in the window together for hours. "Come on, snow!" they **chant**ed. They had never seen it.

Christmas morning they opened their gifts—a brand-new **toboggan** and enough snow **gear** to **outfit** an **excursion** to **Antarctica**. I built a **cheery** fire in the fireplace and told the children to be patient. The snow would come when the snow would come.

New Year's arrived, and still it did not come. Even Marley seemed **antsy**, pacing and gazing out the windows, whimpering softly. The kids returned to school after the holiday, and still nothing. They gazed **sullen**ly at me at the breakfast table. I was the father who had **betray**ed them.

"Maybe little boys and girls in some other place need the snow more than we do," I suggested.

"Yeah, right, Dad," Patrick said.

A couple of weeks later, Patrick came running into our bedroom at dawn and yanked open the blinds. "Look! Look!" he **squeal**ed. "It's here!"

Jenny and I sat up in bed. A white blanket covered the hillsides and cornfields and pine trees and rooftops. "Of course it's here," I answered. "What did I tell you?"

---

chant 같은 말을 반복하다, 노래하다 toboggan 좁고 긴 모양의 썰매 gear (특정활동에 필요한) 장비/복장 outfit (~에) 걸맞く, 장비/복장을 갖추어 주다 excursion 여행, 소풍 Antarctica 남극 cheery 사기를 북돋는, 기운을 나게 하는 antsy 안달하는, 안절부절못하는 sullen 시무룩한, 뚱한 betray 믿음을 저버리다, 배신하다 squeal 비명을 지르듯 큰 소리로 말하다

The snow was nearly a foot deep and still coming down. Soon Conor and Colleen came **chug**ging down the hall, thumbs in mouths, **blankie**s trailing behind them. Sensing the excitement, Marley was up and stretching, banging his tail into everything.

"I guess going back to sleep isn't an option," I told Jenny.

"No, it's not," she said.

"Okay, snow **bunnies**, let's suit up!" I shouted.

For the next half hour we wrestled with zippers and buckles and hats and gloves. By the time we were done, the kids looked like **mummies**.

I opened the front door, and before anyone else could step out, Marley blasted past us, knocking Colleen down. The instant his paws hit the foreign white stuff, he had second thoughts. "Ah, wet! Ah, cold!" He attempted an abrupt **about-face**. But stopping *and* turning at the same time on slippery snow was *not* a good idea.

Marley **went into a full skid**, his rear end spinning out in front of him. He dropped down on his side briefly before bouncing upright again, just in time to somersault down the front porch steps and dive headfirst into a

---

chug (기차가) 칙칙 소리를 내며 움직이다 blankie 아이가 안도감을 얻으려고 껴안는 담요 bunny 토끼(아동어) mummy 미라 about-face 180도 방향전환 go into a full skid 쭉 미끄러지다

snowdrift. When he popped back up a second later, he looked like a giant powdered doughnut. Except for a black nose and two brown eyes, he was completely dusted in white. The **Abominable** Snowdog.

Marley did not know **what to make of** this strange substance. He jammed his nose deep into it and let out a violent **sneeze**. He snapped at it and rubbed his face in it. Then he took off **at full throttle**, racing around the yard in a series of giant, **loping** leaps. Every several feet he tumbled into a somersault or **took a nosedive**. Snow was almost as much fun as raiding the neighbors' trash.

Marley's tracks in the snow told us a lot about his **warped mind**. His path was filled with abrupt twists and turns and about-faces, with **erratic** loops and figure eights, **corkscrew**s, and **triple lutz**es. Soon the kids were following his lead, spinning and rolling and frolicking, snow packing into every crease and crevice of their **outerwear**.

Jenny came out with buttered toast and mugs of hot cocoa. "School's closed," she announced. The first snow day of our children's lives was now perfect.

I scraped the snow away from the stone circle I had

abominable 못난 what to make of A A를 어떻게 생각해야/받아들여야 할지 sneeze 재채기 at full throttle 최대 속도로 lope 성큼성큼 걷다/뛰다 take a nosedive 곤두박질 치다 warped mind 난해한 정신세계/사고방식 erratic 불규칙한 corkscrew 나선형 triple lutz 트리플 러츠 (피겨 스케이팅 기술) outerwear 겉옷

built that fall for backyard campfires and soon had a crackling **blaze** going.

The kids glided screaming down the hill in the toboggan, past the campfire and to the edge of the woods. Marley chased behind.

When the three of them took a break, to get warm by the fire, I decided to try a run on the toboggan.

"Care to join me?" I asked Jenny.

"Sorry, you're on your own," she said.

I positioned the toboggan at the top of the hill and lay back on it, **propped up on** my elbows with my feet tucked inside its nose. I began **rock**ing to get moving. Marley rarely got a chance to look down at me. Lying on my back was like delivering an invitation to him. He crept up close to me and sniffed my face.

"What do you want?" I asked. That was all the welcome he needed. He climbed aboard, straddling me and dropping onto my chest. "Get off me, you big **lug**!" I screamed. But it was too late. We were already creeping forward, gathering speed as we began our **descent**.

"Bon voyage!" Jenny yelled behind us.

Off we went, snow flying, Marley plastered on top of

---

blaze 불길, 불꽃 be propped up on ~에 기대다 rock 전후좌우로 흔들다 lug (덩치 큰) 얼간이
descent 하강

me, licking me all over the face as we headed down the slope. We weighed more than the kids, so we went a lot faster—and a lot farther.

"Hold on, Marley!" I screamed. "We're going into the woods!"

We shot past a large walnut tree, then between two wild cherry trees. We crashed through the **underbrush**, brambles tearing at us. Suddenly I remembered the creek up ahead, still unfrozen. There was a **steep** bank that led down to it. And we were going over. I tried to kick my feet out to use as brakes, but they were stuck.

I wrapped my arms around Marley, squeezed my eyes shut, and yelled, "Whoaaaaaa!"

Our toboggan shot over the bank and dropped out from under us. **In a Scooby-Doo moment**, we hovered in midair for an endless second before falling. But instead of Scooby-Doo, I had a madly salivating Labrador retriever **weld**ed to me. We clung to each other as we crash-landed into a snowbank with a soft *poof* and, hanging half off the toboggan, slid to the water's edge.

Marley was up and prancing around me, eager to do it all over again. But not me.

---

underbrush 덤불 숲 steep 가파른, 비탈진 in a Scooby-Doo moment 만화 영화 스쿠비두의 한 장면처럼 (스쿠비두에서는 공중에 붕 떴다가 추락하는 장면이 자주 등장함) weld 찰싹 들러붙다, 용접해 붙이다 poof 휙

"I'm getting too old for this stuff," I said. In the months ahead it would become clear that Marley was, too.

Our dog had turned nine that first winter in Pennsylvania, and he was slowing down. He still had his **burst**s of **adrenalin-pumped energy**, but the bursts were briefer now and **farther apart**. He was happy to snooze most of the day, and on walks he got tired before I did. That had never happened before.

One late-winter day, I walked him down our hill and up the next one, even steeper than ours. We'd done it many times before, and Marley had always led the charge to the top without really trying. This time, though, he was falling behind.

"Come on, boy. You can do it!" I **coax**ed him along.

Marley just did not have the **oomph** needed to make it to the top. It was like watching a toy slowly wind down as its battery went dead. He stopped and sat down.

"You're not going **soft on me**, are you?" I asked. I leaned over to stroke his face with my gloved hands. He looked up at me, his eyes bright, his nose wet. He was

---

burst 돌발적이고 폭발적인 행동   adrenalin-pumped energy 아드레날린이 촉발한 에너지   farther apart 빈도수가 줄어든, 드문드문 일어나는   coax 구슬리다, 달래다   oomph 힘, 활력   soft on someone ~를 봐주는, 관대하게 대하는

tuckered, but he couldn't have been happier. For Marley, life got no better than this, sitting along the side of a country road on a crisp day with your master.

"If you think I'm carrying you, forget it," I said.

In the bright sunshine, I could see just how much gray had crept into his big yellow face. His whole muzzle and a good part of his brow had turned from **buff** to white. Without us quite realizing it, our eternal puppy had become an old dog.

That's not to say Marley behaved any better. He **was** still **up to all his old tricks**. He just took his time doing them. He still stole food off the children's plates. He still flipped open the lid to the kitchen trash can with his nose and **rummage**d inside. He still strained at his leash. Still swallowed all kinds of household objects. Still drank out of the bathtub and trailed water from his mouth. And when the skies darkened and thunder rumbled, he still **panic**ked. If he was alone when storm clouds rolled in, he still turned **destructive**. One day we arrived home to find Marley all upset—and Conor's mattress **rip**ped open down to the coils.

Over the years, we had come to accept the damage,

---

tuckered (out) 녹초가 된 buff 담황색, 누런색 be up to something (나쁜 짓을) 하다 rummage 뒤지다 panic(panick) 겁에 질리다, 공황상태에 빠지다 destructive 파괴적인, 파괴 행동을 일삼는 rip 찢다

which had become much less frequent now that we were away from Florida's daily storms. In a dog's life, some plaster would fall, some cushions would get ripped open, some rugs would shred. They were costs we came to balance against the joy and laughter and protection and **companionship** he gave us. We could have bought a yacht with what we spent on our dog and all the things he destroyed. We'd take Marley any day. Yachts don't wait by the door all day for your return. And they don't live for the moment they can climb in your lap or ride down the hill with you on a toboggan, licking your face.

companionship 동지애, 우정

Reading Comprehension

1. What did the kids expect to find in Pennsylvania?

a. pencils
b. pens
c. pig pens
d. pennies

2. Which of these did Marley not enjoy about Pennsylvania?

a. jumping in piles of Autumn leaves
b. chasing rabbits
c. playing in the snow
d. thunderstorms

3. Place the following sentences in the correct order.

a. John positioned himself on the toboggan, preparing himself to go down the hill.
b. The toboggan went down the hill gaining speed rapidly.
c. The toboggan crash-landed and slid to a stop.
d. Marley climbed on and straddled John's chest on the toboggan.

4. When did John first realize that Marley was getting old?

a. when his fur started to go grey
b. when he couldn't make it to the top of the hill
c. when he started to take his time doing all the usual things
d. the year he turned ten

Answers: **1.** a **2.** d **3.** a-d-b-c **4.** b

18

Poultry on Parade

That spring we decided to try our hand at animal **husbandry**. We owned two acres in the country now. It only seemed right to share it with a farm animal or two. We just had to figure out which kind.

"A cow would be fun," Jenny suggested.

"A cow?" I asked. "Are you crazy? We don't even have a barn. How can we have a cow? Where would we keep it, in the garage next to the minivan?"

"How about sheep? Sheep are cute," she said.

I shot her my best you're-not-being-practical look.

poultry 가금(닭, 칠면조, 오리, 거위 등) **husbandry** 농사

"A goat?" she asked. "Goats are adorable."
In the end we decided on poultry.

Yes, chickens it was. Jenny had **become friendly with** a mom from school who lived on a farm. She said she'd be happy to give us some chicks from the next clutch of eggs to **hatch**.

Our neighbor, Digger, had a large **coop** of his own in which he kept a **flock** of chickens for both eggs and meat. I told him about our plans. He agreed a few hens around the place made sense.

"Just one word of warning," he said, folding his **meaty** arms across his chest. "Whatever you do, don't let the kids name them. Once you name 'em, they're no longer poultry. They're pets."

"Right," I said. Hens could live fifteen years or more, but they **laid** eggs only in their first couple years. When they stopped laying, they **ended up** in the stewing pot. That was just part of managing a flock.

Digger looked hard at me. "Once you name them, it's all over," he repeated.

"Absolutely," I agreed. "No names."

become friendly with 친구가 되다, 친해지다 hatch 알이 부화하다 coop 우리, 닭장 flock 떼, 무리 meaty 살이 두툼한, 통통한 lay (알을) 낳다 end up 결국 (~한) 상태가 되다

The next evening I pulled into the driveway from work, and the three kids raced out of the house to greet me. Each cradled a newborn chick. Jenny was behind them with a fourth in her hands. Her friend, Donna, had brought the baby birds over that afternoon. They were barely a day old and peered up at me with cocked heads. "Are you my mama?" they seemed to ask.

Patrick was the first to break the news. "I named mine Feathers," he **proclaim**ed.

"Mine is Tweety," said Conor.

"My wicka Wuffy," Colleen chimed in.

I shot Jenny a quizzical look.

"**Fluffy**," Jenny said. "She named her chicken Fluffy."

"Jenny," I protested. "What did Digger tell us? These are farm animals, not pets."

"Oh, get real, Farmer John," she said. "You know as well as I do that you could never hurt one of these. Just look at how cute they are."

"Jenny," I said, the **frustration** rising in my voice.

Jenny held up the fourth chick. "By the way," she said, "meet Shirley."

Feathers, Tweety, Fluffy, and Shirley lived in a box on

proclaim 공언하다, 선언하다 fluffy (털이) 복슬복슬한 frustration 좌절, 실패, 낙담

the kitchen counter. A **lightbulb** dangled above them for warmth. They ate and they **poop**ed and they ate some more. And they grew—fast.

Several weeks after we brought the birds home, something **jolt**ed me awake. It was before dawn. I sat up in bed and listened. From downstairs came a weak, **sickly** call. It was **croaky** and **hoarse**.

"**Cock-a-doodle-do**!" it sounded again. A few seconds ticked past.

Then came an equally sickly reply. "Rook-ru-rookru-roo!"

I shook Jenny. "When Donna brought the **chick**s over, you did ask her to check to make sure they were girls, right?" I said.

"You mean you can do that?" she asked. She rolled back over and fell sound asleep.

It turned out that three of our four "laying hens" were males. And males did not make eggs. Mostly, they made noise.

I thought the constant **crow**ing of our roosters would drive Marley insane. In his younger years, the sweet **chirp** of a single tiny **songbird** in the yard would set him off

on a wild barking **jag** as he raced from one window to the next, hopping up and down on his hind legs. Three crowing roosters a few steps from his food bowl, however, had no effect on him at all. He didn't even seem to know they were there. Each day the crowing grew louder and stronger. At five in the morning, the noise rose up from the kitchen to **echo** through the house. "Cock-a-doodle-dooooo!" Marley slept right through the **racket**.

That's when it first occurred to me that maybe he wasn't just ignoring the crowing. Maybe he couldn't hear it.

I walked up behind him one afternoon as he snoozed in the kitchen. "Marley?" Nothing. I said it louder. "Marley!" Nothing. I **clap**ped my hands and shouted, "MARLEY!" He lifted his head and looked blankly around, his ears up, trying to figure out what his **radar** had detected. I did it again, clapping loudly and shouting his name. This time he turned his head enough to **catch a glimpse of** me standing behind him.

Marley bounced up, tail wagging, happy to see me. "Oh, it's you!" the surprised expression on his face said. He

---

jag (~한 행위에의) 도취/몰두, 한바탕 ~하기   echo 울려 퍼지다, 메아리치다   racket 소음   clap 박수를 치다
radar 레이더   catch(take) a glimpse of 언뜻 (어렴풋이) ~을 보다

bumped up against my legs in greeting and gave me a sheepish look, as if to ask, "What's the idea **sneaking up on** me like that?"

My dog, it seemed, was going deaf.

It all made sense. In recent months, Marley had seemed to ignore me in a way he never had before. I would call for him, and he wouldn't even **glance** my way. I would take him outside before going to bed. He would sniff his way across the yard, **oblivious** to my whistles and calls to get him to turn back. And when he was asleep at my feet in the family room and someone rang the doorbell, he wouldn't even open an eye.

Not that he seemed to mind. Retirement **suit**ed **Marley** just **fine**. His hearing problems did not stop him from taking life easy. And now deafness finally gave him an excuse for **disobey**ing. After all, how could he obey what he couldn't hear? He may have been **thick skulled**, but he was smart enough to figure out how to **use** his deafness **to his advantage**. Drop a piece of steak in his bowl, and he would come trotting in from the next room. He still had the ability to detect the dull, satisfying thud of meat on metal. But when I yelled for him to

---

bump 부딪히다 sneak up on (~에게) 몰래 접근하다, 슬그머니 다가가다 glance 흘끔거리다, 슬쩍 보다 oblivious 까맣게 모르는, 의식하지 못하는 not that ~인 것은 아니다 A suits someone fine A는 ~에게 좋다/괜찮다 disobey 거역하다, 반항하다 thick skulled 머리가 나쁜, 아둔한 use A to one's advantage A를 본인에게 유리하게 이용하다

come, he'd stroll away from me—especially when he had somewhere else he'd rather go. He didn't even glance guiltily over his shoulder like he used to.

"I think the dog's **fool**ing us," I told Jenny.

"His hearing problems do seem to come and go whenever it suits him," she agreed. But every time we tested him, sneaking up, clapping our hands, shouting his name, he would not respond. And every time we dropped food in his bowl, he would come running. He appeared to be deaf to all sounds except the one that was dearest to his heart or, more accurately, his stomach—the sound of dinner.

Marley went through life hungry. We gave him four big **scoop**s of dog chow a day—enough food to keep an entire family of **Chihuahua**s going for a week. We also began giving him table **scrap**s, even though every dog guide we had ever read told us not to. Table scraps programmed dogs to prefer human food to dog chow. (Given the choice between a half-eaten hamburger and dry **kibble**, who could blame them?) Table scraps were a recipe for **chubby** canines.

Not our dog. Marley had many problems, but **obesity**

---

fool 속이다 scoop 스푼이나 용기 따위로 한 번 푼 양 Chihuahua 치와와 scrap 음식 찌꺼기/부스러기
kibble 곡식 알갱이, 개 먹이 chubby 통통한 obesity 비만

was not one of them. No matter how many calories he **devour**ed, he always burned more. All that **high-strung** exuberance ate up lots of energy. He was like a high-kilowatt electric plant that instantly converted every ounce of available fuel into pure, raw power.

Marley was an amazing physical **specimen**, the kind of dog passersby stopped to admire. He was huge for a Labrador retriever, considerably bigger than the average male of his breed, which weighs between sixty-five and eighty pounds. Marley was ninety-seven pounds of pure muscle. We were not worried about him getting fat.

Each evening after the family finished dinner, I filled Marley's bowl with chow, then freely tossed in any tasty leftovers or scraps I could find. With three young children at the table, we had plenty of half-eaten food. Bread crusts, steak **trimming**s, pan **dripping**s, chicken skin, **gravy**, rice, carrots, **pureed prune**s, sandwiches, three-day-old pasta. Into the bowl it went. We kept **dairy** products, sweets, potatoes, and chocolate from him because those were unhealthy for dogs. But that was just about all he couldn't have.

When Marley wasn't acting as our household **garbage**

---

devour 게걸스럽게 삼키다, 먹어치우다 high-strung 쉽게 흥분하는 specimen 표본 trimming 음식 찌꺼기 dripping 고기 기름 gravy 그레이비(육수로 만든 소스) pureed prune 자두 퓌레 dairy 유제품의 garbage disposal 음식물 찌꺼기 처리기

disposal, he was on duty as the family's emergency spill **response team**. No mess was too big a job for our dog. One of the kids would flip a full bowl of spaghetti and meatballs on the floor, and we'd simply whistle and stand back as Old Wet **Vac** sucked up every last noodle. Then he would lick the floor until it gleamed. Escaped peas, dropped **celery**, runaway **rigatoni**, spilled applesauce, it didn't matter what it was. If it hit the floor, it was history. To the amazement of our friends, he even wolfed down salad greens.

Not that food had to make it to the ground before it ended up in Marley's stomach. He was a skilled and **unremorseful** thief. Unsuspecting children were his favorite target—after he checked to make sure neither Jenny nor I was watching.

Birthday parties were **bonanza**s for him. He would make his way through the crowd of five-year-olds, shamelessly **snatch**ing hot dogs right out of their hands. During one party, we estimated he ended up getting two-thirds of the birthday cake, **nab**bing piece after piece off the paper plates the children held on their laps.

It didn't matter how much food he devoured, either

---

response team 대책반 vac 진공청소기 celery 셀러리 rigatoni (파스타) 리가토니 unremorseful 뉘
우침이 없는, 뻔뻔한 bonanza 노다지, 횡재 snatch 낚아채다, 잡아채다 nab 낚아채다

through **legitimate** means or theft. He always wanted more.

One day I arrived home from work to find the house empty. Jenny and the kids were out somewhere.

"Marley," I called. No response.

I walked upstairs, where he sometimes snoozed, but he was nowhere in sight. After I changed my clothes, I returned downstairs and found him in the kitchen up to no good. With his back to me, he was standing on his hind legs. His front paws and chest rested on the kitchen table as he gobbled down the remains of a grilled cheese sandwich. I decided to see how close I could get before he realized he had company. I **tiptoe**d up behind him until I was close enough to touch him. As he chewed the crusts, he kept glancing at the door that led into the garage. He knew that was where Jenny and the kids would enter when they returned. The instant the door opened, he would be on the floor under the table, pretending to be asleep. He hadn't figured out that Dad would be arriving home, too, and just might sneak in through the front door.

"Oh, Marley?" I asked in a normal voice. "What do you

legitimate 정당한, 타당한   tiptoe 까치발로 걷다

think you're doing?" He just kept **gulp**ing the sandwich down, **clueless** to my presence. His tail was wagging lazily, a sign he thought he was alone and getting away with a major food **heist**. He clearly was pleased with himself.

I **cleared my throat** loudly, and he still did not hear me. I made kissy noises with my mouth. Nothing. He **polished off** one sandwich, nosed the plate out of the way and stretched forward to reach the crusts left on a second plate.

"You are such a bad dog," I said as he chewed away.

I snapped my fingers twice and he froze **midbite**, staring at the back door. "What was that? Did I hear a car door **slam**?" After a moment, he decided that whatever he had heard was nothing and went back to his stolen snack.

That's when I reached out and tapped him once on the butt. I might as well have **lit off** a stick of dynamite. The old dog nearly jumped out of his fur coat. He **rocket**ed backward off the table. As soon as he saw me, he dropped onto the floor, rolling over to expose his belly to me in surrender.

---

gulp 게걸스럽게 먹다/마시다 clueless 까맣게 모르는, 우둔한 heist 강도질 clear one's throat 헛기침을 하다 polish off 전부/싹 먹어치우다 midbite 먹는/씹는 중간에 slam 쾅 닫다 light off 불을 붙이다 rocket 쏜살같이 움직이다, 튀어나오(가)다

"**Busted**!" I told him. "You are so busted." But I didn't have it in me to scold him. He was old. He was deaf. He would never **reform**. I wasn't going to change him. Sneaking up on him had been great fun, and I laughed out loud when he jumped. Now as he lay at my feet begging for forgiveness I just found it a little sad. I guess secretly I had hoped he had been faking all along.

I built a chicken coop so our newest family members could safely live outside. Donna kindly took back two of our three roosters and exchanged them for hens from her flock. We now had three girls and one **loudmouth** guy bird.

We let the chickens out each morning to **roam** the yard, and Marley made a few **gallant** runs at them. He charged ahead, barking as he ran about a dozen paces. Then he'd lose **steam** and give up. Something deep inside him said, "You're a retriever; they are birds. Don't you think it might be a good idea to chase them?" But his heart just wasn't in it.

Soon the birds learned the lumbering yellow beast was no threat—more a minor annoyance than anything

busted 체포된, 딱 걸린 reform 나아지다 loudmouth 떠버리, 쓸데없는 말이 많은 사람 roam 돌아다니다, 배회하다 gallant 용맹한 steam 에너지, 의지

else. Marley learned to share the yard with these new, feathered **interloper**s. One day I looked up from weeding in the garden to see Marley and the four chickens making their way down the row toward me as if in formation. The birds **peck**ed and Marley sniffed as they went. It was like old friends out for a Sunday stroll.

"What kind of self-respecting hunting dog are you?" I scolded him. Marley lifted his leg and **pee**d on a tomato plant before hurrying to rejoin his new pals.

interloper 침입자 peck (부리로) 쪼다

Reading Comprehension

1. What is animal husbandry?

a. match-making for animals
b. raising and breeding farm animals
c. domesticating animals for living together
d. counseling animals on marriage

2. Why did Digger warn John not to name his chickens?

a. The Grogans already had too many pets in the house.
b. The chickens will die if they are named.
c. To avoid being too attached to them as pets
d. Chickens with names don't lay eggs.

3. Match Marley's response to each action.

a. John is whistling and calling for Marley. (   )
b. Somebody rings the doorbell. (   )
c. A piece of steak is dropped on the floor. (   )
d. Marley is caught stealing food from the table. (   )

1) Marley comes in right away to eat it.
2) Marley rolls over onto his back.
3) Marley continues to sniff the yard.
4) Marley continues sleeping.

4. Choose the correct word.

Every night I filled Marley's bowl with chow and (water/scraps). With three (children/chickens), we had plenty of half-eaten food. Bread crusts, steak trimmings, pan drippings, sandwiches and three-day-old pasta went into the (bowl/bin).

Answers: **1.** b **2.** c **3.** a-3, b-4, c-1, d-2 **4.** scraps, children, bowl

19

The Potty Room

Marley aged about seven years for every one of ours. In human years, he was close to ninety. His once **sparkling** white teeth had gradually **worn down** to brown **nub**s. Three of his four front fangs were missing, broken off one by one during crazed panic attacks as he tried to chew his way to China. His breath was always a bit **on the fishy side**. Now it had taken on the scent of **rot**ting garbage. It didn't help that he had taken to gobbling up chicken **manure** like it was **caviar**.

Marley's digestion was not what it once had been, and

potty 아기용 변기   sparkling 반짝거리는   wear down 닳다, 닳아 없어지다   nub 덩어리, 조각   fishy 비린 내가 나는   on the ~ side ~한 편인, 다소 ~한   rot 썩다, 부패하다   manure 비료, 거름   caviar 캐비아(철 갑상어의 알을 소금에 절인 것)

he became as **gassy** as a **methane plant**. There were days I swore if I lit a match the whole house would **go up**. Marley was able to clear an entire room with one silent, deadly **fart**. The more visitors we had, the more he let them **rip**.

"Marley! Not again!" the children would scream in unison and lead the **retreat** out of the room.

Sometimes he **drove** even himself **away**. He would be sleeping peacefully when the smell would reach his nostrils. His eyes would pop open and he'd scrunch up his brow as if asking, "Who **dealt** *that*?" Then he would stand up and casually move into the next room.

When Marley wasn't farting, he was outside pooping. Or at least thinking about it. Each time I let him out, he took longer and longer to decide on just the perfect spot. Back and forth he would walk. Round and round he went, sniffing, pausing, scratching, circling, and moving on. The entire time he wore a ridiculous grin on his face. I stood outside, sometimes in the rain, sometimes in the snow, sometimes in the dark of night, often **barefoot**, occasionally just in my underwear. I didn't dare leave him unsupervised or he might head up the hill to visit the

---

gassy 배에 가스가 가득 찬 methane plant 메탄 공장 go up 폭발하다, 불에 타다 fart 방귀 rip 재빨리 꽁무니를 빼다, 전속력으로 달려가다 retreat 피신, 후퇴 drive away 내쫓다, 몰아내다 deal (타격을) 입히다, 가하다 barefoot 맨발의, 맨발로

dogs on the next street.

Sneaking away became a sport for him. If he had the chance and thought he could get away with it, he would bolt for the property **line**. Well, not exactly bolt. He would sniff and **shuffle** his way from one bush to the next until he was out of sight.

Late one night, I let him out the front door for his final walk of the night. Freezing rain was falling, forming an icy **slush** on the ground. I turned around to grab a raincoat out of the front closet. When I walked out on the sidewalk less than a minute later, he was nowhere to be found. I went into the yard, whistling and clapping, knowing he couldn't hear me, but I was pretty sure all the neighbors could. For twenty minutes, I **prowl**ed through our neighbors' yards in the rain—dressed in boots, raincoat, and boxer shorts. I prayed no porch lights would come on. The more I hunted, the angrier I got. But as the minutes passed, my anger turned to worry.

I returned home and woke up Jenny. "Marley's disappeared," I said. "I can't find him anywhere. He's out there in the freezing rain."

Jenny was on her feet instantly, pulling on jeans,

line 경계선 shuffle 발을 질질 끌며 걷다 slush 녹기 시작해서 질퍽해진 눈 prowl 살금살금 돌아다니다, 배회하다

slipping into a sweater and boots. Together we broadened the search. I could hear her way up the side of the hill, whistling and **cluck**ing for him as I crashed through the woods in the dark.

Eventually our paths met up. "Anything?" I asked.

"Nothing," Jenny said. We were soaked from the rain, and my bare legs were **sting**ing from the cold.

"Come on," I said. "Let's go home and get warm and I'll come back out with the car." We returned down the hill and up the driveway.

That's when we saw him, standing beneath the **overhang** out of the rain and overjoyed to have us back. I could have killed him. Instead I brought him inside and toweled him off. The **unmistakable** smell of wet dog filled the kitchen. Exhausted from his late-night jaunt, Marley **conked out** and did not budge till nearly noon the next day.

Marley's eyesight had grown **fuzzy**. Bunnies scampered just a dozen feet away, and he didn't notice. He shed huge amounts of fur. Dog hair made its way into every crevice of our home, every piece of our clothing, and more than

---

slip into 옷을 재빨리 입다   cluck 혀를 차서 (동물을 부르는) 쯧쯧 소리를 내다   sting 얼얼하다, 욱신욱신 쑤시다   overhang 벽보다 튀어나온 지붕이나 위층의 부분   unmistakable 틀릴 수가 없는, 명백한   conk out 잠들다, 뻗다   fuzzy 흐릿한

a few of our meals. He would shake and a cloud of loose fur would rise around him, drifting down onto every surface. One night as I watched television, I dangled my leg off the couch and absently stroked his hip with my bare foot. At the commercial break, I looked down to see a **sphere** of fur the size of a grapefruit near where I had been rubbing. His hairballs rolled across the wood floors like **tumbleweed**s on a windblown plain.

Most **worrisome** of all were his hips. **Arthritis** had snuck into his joints, making them weak and achy. When he was young, I used to ride on his back like a cowboy on a horse. He had lifted the entire dining-room table on his shoulders and bounced it around the room. Now he could barely pull himself up. He groaned in pain when he lay down, and **groan**ed again when he struggled to his feet. I did not realize just how weak his hips had become until one day when I gave his rump a light pat. His hindquarters collapsed beneath him as though he had just received a cross-body block. Down he went. It was painful to watch.

Climbing the stairs to the second floor was tough, too. But Marley would not think of sleeping alone on the

---

sphere 구(球), 공 tumbleweed 회전초 worrisome 걱정되는, 우려되는 arthritis 관절염 groan 끙 하는 신음 소리를 내다

main floor, even after we put a dog bed at the foot of the stairs for him. He loved people, loved being **underfoot**, loved resting his chin on the mattress and panting in our faces as we slept. He loved jamming his head through the shower curtain for a drink as we bathed, and he wasn't about to stop now. Each night when Jenny and I went to bed, he would **fret** at the foot of the stairs, whining, **yip**ping, and pacing.

"Come on, boy. You can do it," I called from the top of the stairs. After several minutes of this, he would disappear around the corner in order to get a running start and then come charging up. Sometimes he made it. Sometimes he got only halfway and had to return to the bottom and try again. On his most pitiful attempts, he would lose his **footing** entirely and slide backward down the steps on his belly. He was too big for me to carry, so I followed him up the stairs, lifting his rear end up each step as he hopped forward on his front paws.

Did all of this trouble stop Marley? Not a chance. That would be **giving** him far too much **credit for** common sense. No matter how much trouble he had getting up the stairs, if I returned downstairs, he would be right on my heels, **clomp**ing heavily down behind me. I might only have to grab a book or turn off the lights. So seconds later he would have to repeat the torturous climb again. Jenny and I started sneaking around behind his back once he was upstairs for the night. We didn't want him to follow us back down. It hardly ever worked. He always seemed to know when we had **snuck off**.

I would be reading in bed and he would be asleep on the floor beside me, snoring heavily. Slowly, I would pull back the covers, slide out of bed, and tiptoe past him out of the room, turning back to make sure I had not disturbed him. I would be downstairs for only a few seconds when I would hear his heavy steps on the stairs, coming in search of me. He might be deaf and half blind, but Marley's radar worked just fine.

This went on all day long, too. I would be reading the newspaper at the kitchen table with Marley curled up **at my feet**. I'd get up for a refill from the coffeepot across the room. I was within sight and would be coming right back, but Marley didn't know it. Very slowly he would get on his feet and **trudge** over to be with me. Just as he got comfortable at my feet by the coffeepot, it would be time

---

clomp 쿵쿵거리며 걷다 **sneak off** 슬그머니 사라지다 **at someone's feet** ~의 발치에서 **trudge** 느릿느릿 터덜거리며 걷다

for me to return to the table. So he would again drag himself up and settle in next to me. A few minutes later, I would walk into the family room to turn on the stereo. He would struggle up again. He'd follow me in, then circle around and collapse with a **moan** beside me—just as I was ready to walk away.

Marley had good days and bad days. He had good minutes and bad minutes, too. They happened so close together, sometimes it was hard to believe it was the same dog.

One evening in the spring of 2002, I took Marley out for a short walk around the yard. The night was cool and windy. I started to run, and Marley galloped along beside me just like in the old days.

"See, Marl, you still have some of the puppy in you," I told him. We trotted together back to the front door, his tongue out as he panted happily, his eyes alert.

Marley tried to leap up the two **porch** steps—but his rear hips collapsed on him as he pushed off. He was **stuck**. With his front paws on the **stoop**, his belly rested on the steps and his butt collapsed flat on the sidewalk.

moan 끙 하는 신음 소리 porch 건물 밖의 현관 stuck 오도 가도 못하는, 꼼짝 못하는 stoop 현관 계단

There he sat, looking up at me like he didn't know what had caused such an **embarrassing display**. I whistled and slapped my hands on my thighs. Using all his might, he flailed his front legs, trying to get up. But it was no use. He could not lift his rear off the ground.

"Come on, Marley!" I called, but he was **immobilized**. Finally I grabbed him under the front shoulders and turned him sideways so he could get all four legs on the ground. After a few tries, he was able to stand up. He backed up, looked at the stairs for a few seconds, and loped up and into the house. From that day on, his confidence as a champion stair climber was shot. He never attempted those two small steps again without first stopping and fretting.

No doubt about it, getting old was no fun. No fun at all.

By November 2002, I had found another new job, writing for the *Philadelphia Inquirer*. I had been in the new job only a few months when the first big snowstorm of 2003 hit.

---

embarrassing 난처한, 곤란한, 창피한 display 쇼, 구경거리 immobilized 움직일 수 없는, 꼼짝할 수 없는

The **flake**s began to fall on a Sunday night, and by the time they stopped the next day, a blanket two feet deep covered the ground. The children were **off school** for three days. With a **snowblower** borrowed from my neighbor, I cleared the driveway and opened a narrow **canyon** to the front door. I knew Marley could never climb the steep walls to get out into the yard, let alone make his way through the deep **drift**s once he was off the path. So I cleared a small space off the front walkway where he could do his business. The kids called it his potty room.

I called him outside to try it out. He just stood in the clearing and sniffed the snow suspiciously. He had very particular ideas about where he could and could not go. This clearly was not what he had in mind. He was willing to lift his leg and pee, but that's where he **drew the line**. He looked up at me as if to say, "Poop right here? **Smack** in front of the **picture window**? You can't be serious." He turned away and went back inside.

That night after dinner I brought him out again. This time Marley couldn't wait. He had to go. He nervously paced up and down the cleared walkway, into the potty

---

flake 눈송이 off school 학교에 가지 않는 snowblower 제설기, 눈 치우는 기계 canyon 깊은 골짜기, 협곡 drift (바람에 의해 쌓인) 눈 더미 draw the line 거부하다, 한계를 설정하다 smack 정확하게, 정통으로 picture window 전망창

room and out onto the driveway. Sniffing the snow and **paw**ing at the frozen ground was his way of saying, "No, this just won't do."

Before I could stop him, he somehow **scramble**d up and over the snow wall the snowblower had cut. He began making his way across the yard toward a **stand** of white pines fifty feet away. I could not believe it. My arthritic old dog was **off on an alpine trek**. Every couple steps his back hips collapsed on him and he sank down into the snow. There he rested on his belly for a few seconds before struggling back to his feet and **pushing on**. Slowly, painfully, he made his way through the deep snow, using his **still-strong** front shoulders to pull his body forward. I stood in the driveway, wondering how I was going to rescue him when he finally got stuck and could go no farther. But he trudged on and finally made it to the closest pine tree. Suddenly I saw what he was **up to**. The dog had a plan.

Beneath the dense branches of the pine, the snow was just a few inches deep. The tree acted like an umbrella. Marley was free to move about and squat comfortably to **relieve himself**. I had to admit, it was pretty brilliant. He

---

paw 발로 긁다/건드리다 scramble 후다닥 기어오르다 stand 한 종류의 나무들로 이루어진 숲 off (길을) 떠나는 alpine 알프스 산의, 산의 trek 고된 여행 on a trek 여행을 하는/하여 push on 계속하다, 밀고 나가다 still-strong 여전히 튼튼한 up to ~한 일을 꾸미고 있는 relieve oneself 배설하다

circled and sniffed and scratched in his **customary** way, trying to **locate** a worthy **shrine** for his daily **offering**. Then, to my amazement, he abandoned the **cozy** shelter and lunged back into the deep snow, on his way to the next pine tree. The first spot looked perfect to me, but clearly it wasn't up to his standards.

The second tree was also tough for Marley to get to. But after a lot of circling, he again decided the area beneath its branches wasn't quite right. So he set off to the third tree, and then the fourth and the fifth, each time getting farther from the driveway. I tried calling him back, though I knew he could not hear me.

"Marley, you're going to get stuck, you **dumbo**," I yelled. He just **plow**ed ahead. The dog was **on a quest**. Finally he reached the last tree on our property, a big **spruce** with a dense **canopy** of branches. It was near where the kids waited for the school bus. Here he found the frozen piece of ground he had been looking for, private and barely dusted with snow. He circled a few times and creakily squatted down on his old, shot, arthritis-riddled haunches. There he finally found relief. **Eureka**!

---

customary 습관적인 locate ~의 위치를 찾다/파악하다 shrine 성지(聖地) offering 공물, 제물 cozy 아늑한, 포근한 dumbo 멍청이 plow 힘들게 나아가다 on a quest 찾는, 탐색하는 spruce 가문비나무 canopy 지붕이나 차양, 늘어진 나뭇가지처럼 위쪽에 드리워진 것 eureka (감탄사) 바로 이거야! 됐어!

With mission accomplished, he set off on the long journey home.

"Keep coming, boy!" I called. "You can make it!" As he struggled through the snow, I waved my arms and clapped my hands to encourage him. But I could see him tiring, and he still had a long way to go. "Don't stop now," I yelled.

A dozen yards from the driveway, that's just what he did. He was done. He stopped and lay down in the snow, exhausted. Marley did not exactly look **distressed**, but he did not look at ease, either. He shot me a worried look that said, "Now what do we do, boss?"

I had no idea. I could wade through the snow to him, but then what? He was too heavy for me to pick up and carry. For several minutes, I stood there, calling and **cajoling**, but Marley would not budge.

"Hang on," I said. "Let me get my boots on and I'll come get you." I grabbed the toboggan, figuring I could wrestle him up onto it and pull him back to the house.

But as soon as he saw me approaching with the toboggan, Marley suddenly jumped up, **reenergize**d. He must have remembered our ride into the woods and over

distressed 괴로운, 고통스러운, 힘든   cajole 꼬드기다, 부추기다   reenergize 기운을 되찾다

the creek bank. He was probably hoping to do it again. He lurched forward toward me like a dinosaur in a **tar pit**. I waded out into the snow, stomping down a path for him as I went, and he inched ahead. Finally we scrambled over the snowbank and onto the driveway together. He shook off the snow and banged his tail against my knees, prancing about, all frisky and **cocky**, **flush** with the **bravado** of an adventurer just back from a **jaunt** through **uncharted wilderness**. To think I had doubted he could do it.

The next morning I shoveled a narrow path out to the far spruce tree on the corner of the property for him. Marley **adopt**ed the space as his own personal toilet for the rest of the winter. The crisis had been **avert**ed, but bigger questions **loom**ed. How much longer could he continue on like this? And at what point would the aches of old age **outstrip** the happiness he found in each sleepy, lazy day?

tar 콜타르, 타르 pit 구덩이 cocky 우쭐한 flush ~로 가득한 bravado 허세 jaunt 나들이, 짧은 여행 uncharted 지도 상에 없는 wilderness 오지, 황무지 adopt ~으로 삼다, 채택하다 avert (안 좋은 일이 일어나는 것을) 막다, 피하다 loom 위협적으로 나타나다(떠오르다) outstrip 앞지르다, 능가하다

Reading Comprehension

1. Match the parts of Marley to the correct description.

a. teeth
b. breath
c. fur
d. eyesight

1) fuzzy and no longer as sharp as it used to be
2) worn down to brown nubs
3) fishy and stinky like garbage
4) falling out everywhere

2. Choose the correct word.

Marley loved people, (loved/hated) being underfoot, loved resting his (chin/tail) on the mattress and panting in our faces as we slept. He loved jamming his head through the shower curtain for a (bath/drink) as we bathed, and he wasn't about to (drop/stop) now.

3. What was Marley looking for beneath the pine trees?

a. something to eat
b. a place to dig
c. somewhere to poop
d. somewhere to sleep

4. How did John feel about Marley's old age?

a. sad and worried
b. happy and excited
c. relieved and expectant
d. calm and indifferent

Answers: **1.** a-2, b-3, c-4, d-1 **2.** loved, chin, drink, stop **3.** c **4.** a

20
Beating the Odds

When school **let out** for the summer, Jenny packed the kids into the minivan and headed to Boston for a week to visit her sister. I stayed behind to work. With Jenny and the kids away, I knew I would be putting in long days. We decided to board Marley at the local **kennel** we used every summer when we went on vacation.

"Waddy go doggie camp!" Colleen screeched.

Marley **perked up** as though he thought Colleen had a pretty good idea. We joked about the activities the kennel staff would have for him—hole digging from nine to ten,

odds 확률, 가능성 beat the odds 불가능을 이기다, 드문 일이 일어나다 let out 끝나다 kennel 개를 맡아 돌보아주는 시설, 애견 훈련소 perk up 기운을 차리다

pillow shredding from 10:15 to eleven, garbage raiding from 11:05 to noon. The truth was, Marley never seemed to relax when he was at the kennel. I always worried a little about him.

I **dropped him off** on a Sunday evening and left my cell-phone number with the front desk. On Tuesday morning of that week, I was seeing the sights in downtown Philadelphia when my cell phone rang.

"Hello?" I answered.

"Could you please hold for Dr. Hopkinson?" the woman from the kennel asked. A few seconds later the vet came on the phone.

"We have an emergency with Marley," she said.

My heart rose in my chest. "An emergency?"

Dr. Hopkinson said Marley's stomach had **bloat**ed with food, water, and air. It had flipped over on itself, twisting and **trap**ping its contents. With nowhere for the gas and other contents to escape, his stomach had swelled painfully, in a **life-threatening** condition.

"It almost always requires surgery to correct," she said. She added that a dog could die if the problem wasn't **fix**ed.

<small>drop someone off 데려다 주다, 맡기다 bloat 붓다, 부풀어 오르다 trap 가두다 life-threatening 생명을 위협하는 fix 고치다, 해결하다</small>

The vet said she had inserted a tube down Marley's throat and released much of the gas that had **built up** in his stomach. That **relieve**d the **swelling**. By **manipulating** the tube in his stomach, she thought she had **worked the twist out of his stomach**, or as she put it, "unflipped it." Now he was **sedate**d and resting comfortably.

"That's a good thing, right?" I asked cautiously.

"But only temporary," the doctor said. "We got him through the **immediate** crisis, but once their stomachs twist like that, they almost always will twist again."

"Like how almost always?" I asked.

"I would say he has a one percent chance that it won't flip again," she said.

"One percent? That's it?"

"I'm sorry," she said. "It's very **grave**."

If his stomach did flip again, we had two choices. The first was to **operate** on him.

"The operation will cost about two thousand dollars," she said. I **gulp**ed. "And I have to tell you, it's very **invasive**. It will be tough going for a dog his age." The recovery would be long and difficult—assuming he

---

build up 늘어나다, 증가하다 relieve 덜다, 완화하다 swelling 부기 manipulate 조종하다, 능숙하게 다루다 work the twist out of the stomach 꼬인 위장을 풀다 sedate 진정제를 놓다 immediate 당면한 grave 심각한 operate 수술하다 gulp (놀라거나 공포심을 느껴) 헉 숨을 들이마시다 invasive 몸에 칼을 대는, 외과적인

made it through the operation at all. Sometimes older dogs like him did not survive the **trauma** of the surgery, she explained.

"If he were four or five years old, I would be saying by all means let's operate," the vet said. "But at his age, you have to ask yourself if you really want to **put him through** that."

"**Not if we can help it**," I said. "What's the second option?"

"The second option," she said, hesitating only slightly, "would be **putting him to sleep**."

"Oh," I said.

I was having trouble **process**ing it all. Five minutes ago, I was walking to the Liberty Bell assuming Marley was resting in his kennel **run**. Now I was being asked to decide whether he would live or die. I had never even heard of the condition she described. Later I learned that bloat was fairly common in some breeds of dogs, especially those with deep **barrel chest**s. Dogs who **scarfed down** their entire meal in a few quick gulps also seemed to be at higher risk. Marley definitely fit the description.

---

make it through 이겨내다, 극복하다 trauma 충격적인 경험 put someone through A(unpleasant experience) A로 고생을 시키다 Not if we can help it 되도록 피하고 싶다, 피할 수 있다면 그러지 않겠다 put someone to sleep 안락사시키다 process 다루다, 받아들이다 run 동물 우리 barrel chest 딱 벌어진 가슴 scarf down 게걸스럽게 삼키다

Dr. Hopkinson agreed that Marley's excitement around the other dogs in the kennel could have **brought on** the attack. He had gulped down his food as usual, and was panting and salivating heavily, **worked up** by all the other dogs around him. All that might have caused the problem.

"Can't we just wait and see how he does?" I asked. "Maybe it won't twist again."

"That's what we're doing right now—waiting and watching," she said. "If his stomach flips again, I'll need you to make a quick decision. We can't let him suffer."

"I need to speak with my wife," I told her. "I'll call you back."

I called Jenny on her cell phone and explained the situation. There was silence on the other end.

"Hello? Are you still there?" I asked.

"I'm here," Jenny said, then went quiet again. By the end of the conversation, we decided there was really no decision at all. The vet was right. Marley was thirteen years old and **fading on all fronts**. It would be cruel to put him through **traumatic** surgery. No matter what, he was close to the end of his life. If this was Marley's time, then it was his time. It was our responsibility to make sure he didn't suffer. We knew it was the right thing—even though neither of us was ready to lose him.

I called the veterinarian back and told her our decision. "His teeth are rotted away, he's **stone deaf**, and his hips have gotten so bad he can barely get up the porch stoop anymore," I explained. "He's having trouble squatting to have a bowel movement."

Dr. Hopkinson **made it easy on me**. "I think it's time," she said.

"I guess so," I answered, but I did not want her to **put him down** without calling me first. I wanted to be there with him if possible. "And," I reminded her, "I'm still **holding out for** that one-percent miracle."

"Let's talk in an hour," she said.

An hour later, Dr. Hopkinson sounded slightly more optimistic. Marley was still **holding his own**. **Nourishment** dripped into his body through a tube in his front leg. She raised his odds to five percent. "I don't want you to get your hopes up," she said. "He's a very sick dog."

The next morning, the doctor sounded brighter still.

---

stone deaf 전혀 못 듣는 make it easy on someone ~을 도와주다, 거들다 put down (동물을) 안락사시키다 hold out for A A를 기다리며 결정을 유보하다/버티다 hold one's own 버티다, 저항하다 nourishment 영양분, 자양분

"He had a good night," she said. When I called back at noon, she had removed the tube from his paw and started him on a **soupy** mix of rice and meat. "He's **famished**," she reported.

By the next call, Marley was up on his feet. "Good news," the vet said. "One of our **tech**s just took him outside and he pooped and peed." I **cheer**ed into the phone as though he had just finished first in the dog show. "He must be feeling better," she added. "He just gave me a big sloppy kiss on the lips." Yep, that was our Marley.

"Yesterday I didn't think it was possible," the doc said. "But I think you'll be able to take him home tomorrow."

The following evening after work, that's just what I did. He looked terrible—weak and **skeletal**. His eyes were **milky** and **crusted with mucus**.

"The whole staff loves Marley," the doctor told me. "Everyone was **rooting for** him."

I walked him out to the car. My miracle dog had beaten the odds.

"Let's get you home where you belong," I said. He just stood there looking **woefully** into the backseat. To him,

---

soupy 수프처럼 걸쭉한 famished 매우 굶주린 tech 기술자, 직원 cheer 환호성을 지르다 skeletal 해골처럼 비쩍 마른, 앙상한 milky 희뿌연 crusted with A A가 말라붙은 mucus 점액 root for (~를) 응원하다, 성원을 보내다 woefully 비통하게, 서글프게

it was as impossible to climb as Mount Olympus. He didn't even try to hop in. I called to one of the kennel workers, who helped me carefully lift him into the car.

I drove him home with a box of medicines and strict instructions. Marley would never again gulp a huge meal **in one sitting**, nor slurp unlimited amounts of water. His days of playing submarine with his snout in the water bowl were over. From now on, he would receive four small meals a day. He'd get small amounts of water— a half cup or so in his bowl at a time. The goal was to keep his stomach calm so it wouldn't twist again. And he wouldn't be staying in a large kennel surrounded by barking dogs ever again. Dr. Hopkinson and I were convinced it was the big reason for his **close call with death**.

That night, after I got him home and inside, I spread a sleeping bag on the floor in the family room beside him. He was still too weak to climb the stairs to the bedroom. I did**n't have the heart to leave** him alone and helpless.

"We're having a **sleepover**, Marley!" I proclaimed, and lay down beside him. I stroked him head to tail until

---

in one sitting 한 번 앉은 자리에서, 한 번에 close call 큰일이 날 뻔한 상황 close call with death 죽을 뻔한 상황 not have the heart to do ~할 만한 용기가 없다 sleepover 외박하기, 한 집에 모여 밤새고 놀기

huge clouds of fur rolled off his back. I wiped the mucus from the corners of his eyes and scratched his ears until he moaned with pleasure.

Jenny and the kids would be home in the morning. She would **pamper** him with frequent **minimeal**s of boiled hamburger and rice. The children would throw their arms around him, unaware of how close they had come to never seeing him again.

Tomorrow the house would be loud and **boisterous** and full of life again. For tonight, it was just the two of us, Marley and me. Lying there with him, his smelly breath in my face, I could not help thinking of our first night together all those years ago when I had brought him home from the **breeder**, a tiny puppy whimpering for his mother. I remembered how I had dragged his box into the bedroom and the way we had fallen asleep together, my arm dangling over the side of the bed to comfort him. Thirteen years later, here we were, still **inseparable**. I thought about his **puppyhood** and adolescence, about the shredded couches and eaten mattresses, about the wild walks and **cheek-to-jowl** dances with the stereo **blaring**. I thought about the

---

pamper 극진히 보살피다. 애지중지하다   minimeal 소량의 음식   boisterous 떠들썩한, 활기가 넘치는   breeder 사육사   inseparable 헤어질/떨어질 수 없는   puppyhood 어린 강아지 시절   jowl 턱밑으로 늘어진 살   cheek-to-jowl (부둥켜안은 채) 볼과 턱밑의 살을 맞대고   blare (소리가) 요란하게 나다

swallowed objects and sweet moments of canine-human friendship. Mostly I thought about what a good and loyal **companion** he had been all these years. What a trip it had been.

"You really scared me, old man," I whispered. He stretched out beside me and slid his snout beneath my arm to encourage me to keep petting him. "It's good to have you home."

Marley and I fell asleep together there, side by side on the floor. His rump was half on my sleeping bag. My arm was draped across his back. He woke me once in the night, his shoulders **flinch**ing, his paws twitching, little baby barks coming from deep in his throat. He was dreaming. Dreaming, I imagined, that he was young and strong again. And running like there was no tomorrow.

companion 동반자, 동료 flinch 움직거리다, 움찔하다

Reading Comprehension

1. Where did the Grogans decide to put Marley while they were on holiday?

a. in the laundry room cage
b. in the garage
c. at the local kennel
d. with a neighbour

2. What emergency did the vet call John about?

a. Marley was being naughty at the kennel.
b. Marley was unwell and needed surgery.
c. Marley was howling and unhappy at the kennel.
d. Marley was eating too much.

3. How did the vet know that Marley was feeling better?

a. He pooped and peed.
b. He was howling.
c. He was playing with the other dogs.
d. He gave the vet a big kiss on the lips.

4. Choose the correct word.

Marley would never again (gulp/nibble) a huge meal in one sitting, nor (sip/slurp) unlimited amounts of water. His days of playing (submarine/airplane) with his snout in the water bowl were over. From now on, he would receive four (large/small) meals a day.

Answers: **1.** c **2.** b **3.** d **4.** gulp, slurp, submarine, small

21

Borrowed Time

Over the next several weeks, Marley **bounced back from the edge of death**. The mischievous **sparkle** returned to his eyes, the cool wetness to his nose, and a little meat to his bones. He was content to snooze his days away in front of the glass door in the family room where the sun **flooded in** and **bake**d his fur.

On his new diet, he was **perpetually** hungry. He begged and stole food more **shamelessly** than ever. One evening I caught him alone in the kitchen, up on his hind legs with his front paws on the kitchen counter,

---

bounce back (from a bad experience) (역경을) 극복하다, 회복하다   **from the edge of death** 죽음의 문턱에서, 사경으로부터   **sparkle** 광채, 번뜩임   **flood in** 쏟아져 들어오다   **bake** 달구다, 덥히다   **perpetually** 영원히, 언제나   **shamelessly** 뻔뻔하게

stealing **Rice Krispies Treats** from a **platter**. How he got up there, I'll never know. He could barely walk on his frail hips, but that didn't stop him. When the **will** called, Marley's body answered. I wanted to hug him, I was so happy at the surprise display of strength.

In many ways, he was still the same happy-go-lucky dog. Each morning after his breakfast, he trotted into the family room to use the couch as a giant napkin. He walked along its length, rubbing his snout and mouth against the fabric as he went and flipping up the cushions in the process. Then he would turn around and come back in the opposite direction so he could wipe the other side. From there he would drop to the floor and roll onto his back, wiggling from side to side to give himself a back rub. He liked to sit and lick the carpeting, as if it had **been coated with** the most **delectable** gravy he had ever tasted.

Marley's daily routine included barking at the mailman, visiting the chickens, staring at the **birdfeeder**, and checking the bathtub faucets for any drips of water he could **lap up**. Several times a day, he flipped up the lid on the kitchen trash can to see what **goodie**s he could

---

Rice Krispies Treats 쌀을 함유한 캔디바 platter 접시 will 의지 be coated with 코팅이 되다
delectable 먹음직한, 군침이 도는 birdfeeder 새 모이통 lap up 혀로 핥아먹다 goodie 맛있는 것, 흥미로운 것

scavenge. On a daily basis, he launched into Labrador evader mode, banging around the house, tail thumping the walls and furniture. And on a daily basis I continued to pry open his jaws and pull out all sorts of odds and ends from the roof of his mouth—potato skins and muffin wrappers, discarded Kleenex and **dental floss**. Even in old age, some things didn't change.

In September 2003 I traveled out of town to work on a column I was writing. After I finished, I called home from the hotel.

"I just want you to know that Marley really misses you," Jenny said.

"Marley?" I asked. "How about the rest of you?"

"Of course we miss you, dingo," she said. "But I mean Marley really, *really* misses you. He's driving us all **bonkers**."

The night before, Marley had paced and sniffed the entire house over and over, looking for me. He **poke**d through every room, looking behind doors and in closets. He struggled to get upstairs. When he couldn't find me there, he came back down again and began his search all

---

scavenge 먹을 것을 찾아 쓰레기를 뒤지다   dental floss 치실   bonkers 제정신이 아닌, 정신이 없는   poke 들쑤시고 다니다

over again.

"He was really **out of sorts**," Jenny said.

Marley even braved the steep, **slippery** wooden basement steps. Once down there, he could not get back up again. He stood yipping and whining until Jenny and the kids came to his rescue, holding him beneath the shoulders and hips and **boosting** him **up** step by step.

At bedtime, instead of sleeping beside our bed as he normally did, Marley **camped out** on the landing at the top of the stairs. That way he'd know if I came out of hiding or arrived home during the night—just in case I had snuck out without telling him. He wasn't **taking any chances**.

That's where Marley was the next morning when Jenny went downstairs to make breakfast. A couple hours passed before it dawned on her that he still had not shown his face, which was highly unusual. He almost always was the first one down the steps each morning, charging ahead of us and banging his tail against the front door to go out. She found him sleeping soundly on the floor tight against my side of the bed. Then she saw why. When she had gotten up, she had pushed her

---

out of sorts 기분이 언짢은, 우울한 slippery 미끄러운 boost up 들어 올리다 camp out 바깥에서 자다, 진을 치다 take a chance 운에 맡기다, 도박을 하다

pillows over to my side of the bed. Beneath the covers, they formed a large lump where I usually slept. With his **Mr. Magoo** eyesight, Marley mistook the pile of feathers for his master.

"He absolutely thought you were in there," Jenny said. "I could just tell he did. He was convinced you were sleeping in!" We laughed together on the phone, and then Jenny said, "You've got to give him points for loyalty."

I did. Devotion had always come easily to our dog.

I had been back from my trip for only a week when the crisis we knew could come at any time arrived. I was in the bedroom getting dressed for work when I heard a big crash. Conor screamed, "Help! Marley fell down the stairs!" I came running and found Marley **in a heap** at the bottom of the long staircase, struggling to get to his feet.

Jenny and I raced to him and ran our hands over his body, gently squeezing his limbs, pressing his ribs, massaging his spine. Nothing seemed to be broken. With a groan, Marley made it to his feet, shook off, and walked away without even **limp**ing. Conor had witnessed the

Mr. Magoo 지독한 근시의 백만장자인 만화/영화 주인공 in a heap 쓰러져 있는 limp 다리를 절다, 절뚝거리다

fall. He said Marley had started down the stairs, but after just two steps realized everyone was still upstairs. So he attempted an about-face. As he tried to turn around, his hips dropped out from beneath him. He tumbled in a freefall down the entire length of the stairs.

"Wow, was he lucky!" I said. "A fall like that could have killed him."

"I can't believe he didn't get hurt," Jenny said. "He's like a cat with nine lives."

But Marley had gotten hurt. Within minutes he was **stiffen**ing up, and by the time I arrived home from work that night, Marley couldn't move. He seemed to be sore everywhere. He couldn't put any weight at all on his front left leg. I could squeeze it without him yelping, and I suspected he had **pulled a tendon**. When he saw me, he tried to struggle to his feet to greet me. It was no use. His left front paw was useless. With his weak back legs, he just had no power to do anything. Marley was down to one good limb. He finally made it up and tried to hop on three paws to get to me. His back legs **caved in**, and he collapsed back to the floor. Jenny gave him an aspirin and held a bag of ice to his front leg. Eternally playful Marley

stiffen 뻣뻣하게 굳다   tendon 힘줄   pull a tendon 힘줄이 늘어나다   cave in 무너지다

kept trying to eat the ice cubes.

By 10:30 that night, he was no better. He hadn't been out to pee since one that afternoon. He had been holding his urine for nearly ten hours. I had no idea how to get him outside and back in again so he could relieve himself. Straddling him and clasping my hands beneath his chest, I lifted him to his feet. Together we **waddle**d our way to the front door. I held him up as he hopped along.

But out on the porch stoop Marley froze. A steady rain was falling, and the porch steps were **slick** and wet. He didn't know what to do.

"Come on," I said. "Just a quick pee and we'll go right back inside." He would have no part of it. I wished I could have persuaded him to just pee right on the porch and be done with it. But I couldn't teach this old dog that new trick.

Marley hopped back inside and stared up at me. He seemed to be apologizing for what he knew was coming. "We'll try again later," I said. Just then he halfsquatted on his three remaining legs and emptied his full **bladder** on the foyer floor. A puddle spread out around him. It was the first time since he was a tiny puppy that Marley had

waddle 뒤뚱뒤뚱 걷다   slick 미끄러운   bladder 방광

peed in the house.

The next morning Marley was better, though still **hobbling** about like an **invalid**. We got him outside, where he peed and pooped without problem. On the count of three, Jenny and I lifted him up the porch stairs to get him back inside.

"I have a feeling that Marley will never go upstairs in this house again," I told her. It was obvious he had climbed his last staircase. From now on, he would have to get used to living and sleeping on the ground floor.

Later that day, I was upstairs working on my computer in the bedroom when I heard a commotion on the stairs. I stopped typing and listened. It was a familiar sound— like a horse was galloping up a **gangplank**. I looked at the bedroom doorway and held my breath. A few seconds later, Marley **pop**ped his head around the corner and came into the room. His eyes brightened when he spotted me. "So there you are!" they said.

"Marley, you made it!" I exclaimed. "You old **hound**! I can't believe you're up here!" He smashed his head into my lap, begging for an ear rub, which I figured he had earned.

hobble 다리를 절다, 절뚝거리다   invalid 병약자   gangplank (배와 육지 사이에 걸쳐 놓는) 건널 판자   pop 갑자기 나타나다   hound 사냥개

Later, as I sat on the floor with him and **scruff**ed his neck, he twisted his head around and **gamely gum**med my wrist in his jaws. It was a sign of the playful puppy still in him. The night before, I had prepared myself for the worst—Marley's death. Today he was panting and pawing and trying to **slime** my hands **off**. Just when I thought his long, lucky **run** was over, he was back.

I pulled his head up and made him look me in the eyes. "You're going to tell me when it's time, right?" I said. It was really more of a statement than a question. I didn't want to have to make the decision on my own. "You'll let me know, won't you?"

scruff 잡다 gamely 투지를 보이며, 용맹하게 gum 잇몸으로 씹다 slime off (~에서) 스르륵 빠져나가다, 슬쩍 도망치다 run 여정

# Reading Comprehension

1. Choose the correct word.

Over the next several weeks, Marley bounced back from the edge of (life/death). The mischievous sparkle returned to his (eyes/nose), and a little meat to his (skin/bones). He was content to (snooze/play) his days away in front of the glass door.

2. Place Marley's morning routine in order.

a. Marley eats breakfast and then goes into the family room.
b. Then he sits and licks the carpet.
c. Then he rolls on his back on the floor.
d. He rubs his snout and mouth along the sofa in one direction and then the other.

3. How did Marley get hurt?

a. His stomach twisted again.
b. He fell down the stairs.
c. He ate something bad for him.
d. He fell over in the snow.

4. What did John prepare himself for?

a. another trip
b. Marley's death
c. another emergency
d. spending all his time downstairs

 1. death, eyes, bones, snooze **2**. a-d-c-b **3**. b **4**. b

22

The Big Meadow

Winter arrived early that year. As the days grew short and the winds howled through the frozen branches, we huddled together in our **snug** home. I **chop**ped and split a winter's **worth** of firewood and **stack**ed it by the back door. Jenny made **hearty** soups and homemade breads, and the children once again sat in the window and waited for the snow to arrive.

I awaited the first snowfall, too, but with a quiet sense of **dread**. I wondered how Marley could possibly make it through another tough winter. The previous one had

snug 포근한, 아늑한   chop 자르다   worth 일정한 몫이나 양, 분량, 치   stack 차곡차곡 쌓다, 재어 놓다
hearty 푸짐한, 영양분이 많은   dread (미래에 일어날 일에 대한) 두려움

been hard enough on him. Since then he'd gotten even weaker. I wasn't sure how he would be able to **navigate ice-glazed** sidewalks, slippery stairs, and a snow-covered yard.

On a **blustery** Sunday night in mid-December, Jenny declared a family movie night. The kids raced to pick out a video, and I whistled for Marley. Together we went outside to fetch a basket of **maple** logs off the woodpile. He poked around in the frozen grass as I loaded up the wood, standing with his face into the wind and his wet nose sniffing the icy air. I clapped my hands and waved my arms to get his attention. He followed me inside, hesitating at the front porch steps before gathering up his courage and lurching forward, dragging his back legs up behind him.

Inside, I got the fire **hum**ming as the kids popped the movie in the VCR. The flames leaped and the heat filled the room. As usual, Marley **claim**ed the best spot for himself, directly in front of the **hearth**. I lay down on the floor a few feet from him and **propped my head on** a pillow, watching the fire more than the movie. Marley didn't want to lose his warm spot, but he couldn't miss

navigate 걷다, 길을 찾다 ice-glazed 표면이 얼거나 얼음으로 뒤덮여 유리 같은 blustery 바람이 세차게 몰아치는 maple 단풍나무 hum 활기를 띠다 claim 차지하다, 얻다 hearth 벽난로 바닥 prop one's head on A A를 베다

his chance. His favorite human was at ground level lying flat on his back, utterly defenseless. Who was the alpha male now? His tail began pounding the floor. Then he started wiggling his way in my direction. He **sashay**ed from side to side on his belly, his rear legs stretched out behind him. Soon he was pressed up against me, **grind**ing his head into my ribs. The minute I reached out to pet him, it was all over. He pushed himself up on his paws, and shook hard, showering me in loose fur. He stared down at me, his **billow**ing jowls hanging right over my face. When I started to laugh, he took this as a green light to advance. Before I quite knew what was happening, he had straddled my chest with his front paws and, in one big freefall, collapsed on top of me in a heap.

"Ugh!" I screamed under his weight. "**Full-frontal** Lab **attack**!" The kids squealed with laughter. Marley could not believe his good fortune. I wasn't even trying to get him off me. He squirmed. He drooled. He licked me all over the face and **nuzzle**d my neck. I could barely breathe under his weight. After a few minutes I slid him half off me, where he remained through most of the movie. His head, shoulder, and one paw rested on my

---

sashay 뽐내며 걷다 grind ~에 대고 문지르다, 비비다 billow 불거지다, 부풀다 full-frontal attack 정면 공격 nuzzle (~을) 문지르다, 파고들다

chest and the rest of him pressed against my side.

I didn't say so to anyone in the room, but I found myself clinging to the moment, knowing there would not be too many more like it. Marley was in the quiet **dusk** of a long and **eventful** life. Looking back on it later, I would recognize that night in front of the fire for what it was, our farewell party. I stroked his head until he fell asleep. Then I stroked it some more.

Four days later, we packed the minivan. Our family was headed to Disney World. It would be the children's first Christmas away from home, and they were wild with excitement. Jenny delivered Marley to the veterinarian's office. She had arranged for him to spend our week away in the **intensive** care unit, where the doctors and workers could keep their eyes on him **around the clock** and he would not be **rile**d by the other dogs.

It was a great family vacation. On the long drive back north we went over the **pros and cons** of each ride, each meal, each swim, each moment. When we were halfway through Maryland, just four hours from home, my cell phone rang. It was one of the workers from the vet's office. Marley was acting **lethargic**, she said, and his hips

---

dusk 황혼 eventful 다사다난한, 파란만장한 intensive 집중적인 around the clock 24시간 내내, 밤낮으로 rile 귀찮게 굴다, 짜증 나게 하다 pros and cons 장점과 단점 lethargic 무기력한, 기운이 없는

had begun to **droop** worse than normal. He seemed to be in discomfort. She said the vet wanted our permission to give him a **shot** and pain medication.

"Sure," I said. "Keep him comfortable, and we'll be there to pick him up tomorrow."

Jenny arrived to bring him home the following afternoon, December 29. Marley looked tired and a little out of sorts, but not ill. As we had been warned, his hips were weaker than ever. A worker helped Jenny lift him up into the minivan. But within a half hour of getting him home, he was **retch**ing. Clear, thick mucus coated his throat, and he was trying to clear it. Jenny let him out in the front yard, and he simply lay on the frozen ground. He could not or would not budge.

Jenny called me at work in a panic. "I can't get him back inside," she said. "He's lying out there in the cold and he won't get up." I left immediately. By the time I got home forty-five minutes later, she had managed to get him to his feet and back in the house. I found him sprawled on the dining-room floor, clearly distressed and clearly not himself.

For thirteen years, it had always been the same. I'd walk

into the house. He'd jump to his feet, stretching, shaking, panting, and banging his tail into everything. Not on this day. His eyes followed me as I walked into the room, but he did not move his head. I knelt down beside him and rubbed his snout. No reaction. He did not try to gum my wrist. He did not want to play. He did not even lift his head. His eyes were far away, and his tail lay **limp** on the floor.

After several minutes, Marley slowly stood up on shaky legs and tried to retch again, but nothing would come out. That's when I noticed his stomach. It looked bigger than usual, and it was hard **to the touch**. **My heart sank**. I knew what this meant. I called the veterinarian's office and described Marley's bloated stomach.

"The doctor says to bring him right in," the receptionist told me.

Jenny and I did not have to say a word to each other. We both understood that the moment had arrived. We prepared the kids, telling them Marley had to go to the hospital. We explained that the doctors were going to try to make him better, but that he was very sick.

As I was getting ready to go, I looked at Jenny and the

---

limp 축 늘어진, 피곤한, 지친 to the touch 손으로 만져보니/만졌을 때 someone's heart sinks 가슴이 철렁 내려앉다, 매우 놀라다

kids. They were **huddle**d around Marley saying their good-byes. They each got to pet him and have a few last moments with him. Still, the kids remained positive that Marley would soon be back, good as new. After all, he'd been there with them their whole lives. He had to return.

"Get all better, Marley," Colleen said in her little voice.

With Jenny's help, I got him into the back of my car. She gave him a last quick hug, and I drove off with him, promising to call as soon as I learned something. He lay on the floor in the backseat with his head resting on the center hump. I drove with one hand on the wheel and the other stretched behind me so I could stroke his head and shoulders.

"Oh, Marley," I just kept saying.

In the parking lot of the animal hospital, I helped him out of the car. He stopped to sniff a tree where the other dogs all pee. Good old Marley was never too sick to be curious. I gave him a minute. Marley loved being outside, and I knew this might be the last time he'd have the chance. Then I tugged gently at his choker chain and led him into the lobby. Just inside the front door, he decided he had gone far enough and **gingerly** let himself

huddle 옹기종기 모이다   gingerly 조심조심

down on the tile floor. When the vet's helpers and I were unable to get him back to his feet, they brought out a **stretcher** and slid him onto it. Then they disappeared with him behind the counter into the examining area.

A few minutes later, the vet came out and led me into an exam room, where she put a pair of X-ray films up on a light board. She showed me how his stomach had swollen to twice its normal size and how the **intestine**s had twisted.

"It's a long **shot**, but I'm going to try to get his stomach back into place," she explained. It was exactly the same one-percent gamble Dr. Hopkinson had given over the summer.

"Okay," I said. "Please give it your best shot." It had worked once. It could work again. I silently hoped everything would be all right.

A half hour later, the vet emerged with a **grim** face. She had tried three times and was unable to open the **blockage**. "At this point, our only real option is to go into surgery," she said, then paused. "Or the most humane thing might be to put him to sleep."

Jenny and I had been through this decision five months

---

stretcher 들것 intestine 장, 창자 shot 시도, 노력 grim 음울한, 침통한 blockage 막힌 상태, 폐색

earlier and had already made the hard choice. We did not want Marley to suffer anymore. He deserved better than that. We knew the right thing to do. Yet now, I stood frozen.

I told the doctor I wanted to step outside to call my wife. On the cell phone in the parking lot, I told Jenny that they had tried everything, but nothing had worked. We sat silently on the phone for a long moment before she said, "I love you, John."

"I love you, too, Jenny," I said.

I walked back inside and asked the doctor if I could have a couple minutes alone with him.

"Take all the time you need," she said.

I found him unconscious on the stretcher on the floor. I got down on my knees and ran my fingers through his fur, the way he liked. I ran my hand down his back. I lifted each **floppy** ear in my hands. I pulled up his lip and looked at his lousy, worn-out teeth. I picked up a front paw and **cupped it in my hand**. Then I dropped my forehead against his and sat there for a long time, as if I could send a message through our two skulls, from my brain to his. I wanted to make him understand some

floppy 늘어진 cup something in one's hand 손을 오므려 쥐다

things.

"You know all that stuff we've always said about you?" I whispered. "What a total pain you are? Don't believe it. Don't believe it for a minute, Marley." He needed to know that, and something more, too. There was something I had never told him, that no one ever had. I wanted him to hear it before he went.

"Marley," I said. "You are a *great* dog."

I found the doctor waiting at the front counter. "I'm ready," I said. My voice was **crack**ing. That surprised me because I had really believed I had been ready for this moment for months. I knew if I said another word I would break down and cry, so I just nodded. She led me back to Marley, and I knelt beside him as she prepared the shot. I cradled his head in my hands.

"Are you okay?" she asked. I nodded yes.

The vet gave him the shot, then listened to his heart. It had slowed way down but not stopped. He was a big dog. She gave him a second shot. A minute later, she listened again and said, "He's gone." She left me alone with him, and I gently lifted one of his eyelids. The doctor was

crack (목소리가) 갈라지다

right. Marley was gone.

I walked out to the front desk and paid the bill. A few minutes later, she and an assistant **wheel**ed out a cart with a large black bag on it and helped me lift it into the back seat. The doctor shook my hand.

"I'm so sorry," she said. "I did my best."

"It was his time," I said, then thanked her and drove away.

In the car on the way home, I started to cry. It only lasted a few minutes. By the time I pulled into the driveway, I was dry-eyed again. I left Marley in the car and went inside where Jenny was sitting up, waiting. The children were all in bed asleep. We would tell them in the morning. We fell into each other's arms and both started **weep**ing. I tried to describe it to her, to assure her he was already deeply asleep when the end came, that there was no panic, no pain. But I couldn't find the words. So we simply **rock**ed each other in our arms. Later, we went outside and together lifted the heavy black bag out of the car and into the garden cart, which I rolled into the garage for the night.

---

wheel (바퀴 달린 것을) 밀다   weep 눈물을 흘리다   rock 앞뒤 혹은 좌우로 흔들리다

Reading Comprehension

1. How did each family member prepare for winter? Match the family member to their preparation.

a. John
b. Jenny
c. the children
d. Marley

1) cooked soups and made bread
2) waited by the window for snow
3) slept by the fire
4) chopped some wood

2. Choose the correct word.

I dropped my (forehead/face) against his and sat there for a (long/short) time, as if I could send a (wish/message) through our two skulls, from my (brain/heart) to his.

3. What were John's last words to Marley?

a. I love you.
b. I'm sorry.
c. You are a great dog.
d. I miss you.

4. When did John start to cry?

a. when he called his wife
b. when Marley died
c. in the car as he was driving home
d. when the vet gave Marley the second injection

Answers: **1.** a-4, b-1, c-2, d-3 **2.** forehead, long, message, brain **3.** c **4.** c

23

Beneath the Cherry Trees

I had trouble sleeping that night. An hour before dawn I slid out of bed and dressed quietly, careful not to wake Jenny. In the kitchen, I drank a glass of water and stepped out into a light, **slushy drizzle**. I grabbed a shovel and **pickax** and walked to the white pines that Marley had made his personal potty the winter before. I had decided to bury him in the pea **patch** beside the pines.

The temperature was in the mid thirties, so the ground wasn't frozen. In the half-dark, I began to dig. Once I was through a thin layer of topsoil, I hit heavy, dense

---

slushy drizzle 진눈깨비 pickax(pickaxe) 곡괭이 patch 작은 땅, 밭

clay **studded with** rocks. The digging was slow and hard. After fifteen minutes, I **peeled off** my coat and paused to catch my breath. After thirty minutes, I was in a sweat. I hadn't even dug down two feet yet. After forty-five minutes, I struck water. The hole began to fill. And fill. Soon a foot of muddy cold water covered the bottom. I fetched a bucket and tried to **bail** it, but more water just **seep**ed in. There was no way I could possibly lay Marley down in that icy **swamp**. No way.

My heart was pounding like I had just run a marathon. Despite the work I had invested in it, I abandoned the hole. I **scout**ed the yard, stopping where the lawn meets the woods at the bottom of the hill. Two big native cherry trees arched above me. These were the same trees Marley and I had narrowly missed on our wild toboggan ride.

"This feels right," I said, and sunk my shovel in the ground between them. Digging went easily. Soon I had an **oval** hole four feet deep. When the hole was done, I went inside and found all three kids up, **sniffling** quietly. Jenny had just told them.

I told them it was okay to cry and that owning a dog

---

studded with ~이 많은, ~투성이인   peel off (옷을) 벗다   bail 퍼내다   seep 새다, 스미다   swamp 늪, 습지   scout 탐색하다, 정찰하다   oval 계란형의, 타원형의   sniffle 훌쩍거리다

always ended with this sadness because dogs just don't live as long as people do. I told them how Marley was sleeping when they gave him the shot and that he didn't feel a thing. He just drifted off and was gone.

"I didn't get to say a real good-bye to him," Colleen said. She thought he would be coming home.

"I said good-bye for all of us," I told her.

Conor showed me something he had made to go in the grave with Marley. It was a drawing of a big red heart. Under the heart, he had written, "To Marley, I hope you know how much I loved you all of my life. You were always there when I needed you. Through life or death, I will always love you. Your brother, Conor Richard Grogan."

Colleen drew a picture of a girl with a big yellow dog and beneath it, with spelling help from her brother, she wrote, "P.S. — I will never forget you."

I went out alone and wheeled Marley's body down the hill. I laid an armful of soft pine **bough**s on the floor of the hole. Then I lifted the heavy body bag off the cart and down into the hole as gently as I could. I opened the bag to see him one last time, and positioned him in

bough 나뭇가지

a comfortable, natural way—just as he might be lying in front of the fireplace, curled up, head tucked around to his side.

"Okay, Big Guy, this is it," I said. I closed up the bag and returned to the house to get Jenny and the kids.

As a family, we walked down to the grave. Conor and Colleen had **seal**ed their notes **back-to-back** in a plastic bag. I placed it right beside Marley's head. Patrick used his jackknife to cut five pine boughs, one for each of us. And one by one, we dropped them in the hole, their scent rising around us. We paused for a moment.

"Marley, we love you," we said all together as if we had **rehearse**d it.

I picked up the shovel and tossed the first scoop of dirt in.

When the hole was half filled, I took a break and we all walked up to the house where we sat around the kitchen table and told funny Marley stories. One minute we were crying. The next we were laughing. Jenny told the story of Marley **going bonkers** during the filming of *The Last Home Run* when a stranger picked up Baby Conor. I told about all the leashes he had chewed and the time he peed

---

seal 단단히 봉하다, 막다   back-to-back 다닥다닥 붙여서, 차곡차곡   rehearse 예행연습을 하다   go bonkers 미치광이처럼 행동하다

on our neighbor's ankle. We described all the things he had destroyed and the thousands of dollars he had cost us. We could laugh about it now.

"Marley's spirit is up in dog heaven now," I told the kids. "He's in a giant golden meadow, running free. And his hips are good again. And his hearing is back, and his eyesight is sharp, and he has all his teeth. He's back in his prime—chasing rabbits all day long."

"And having endless screen doors to crash through," Jenny added. The image of him **barging** his way **oafishly** through heaven made everyone laugh.

In the days immediately after we buried Marley, the whole family went silent. For years we'd loved telling funny Marley stories. Now we couldn't talk about him. It was just too painful.

Colleen had the most trouble. She could not bear to hear his name or see his photo. Tears would well in her eyes and she would **clench her fists** and say angrily, "I don't want to talk about him!"

Every night for thirteen years, Marley was waiting for me

barge 휘젓고 다니다   oafishly 얼간이처럼, 멍청하게   clench one's fist 주먹을 꽉 쥐다

at the door when I came home from work. Walking in now at the end of the day was the most painful part of all. The house seemed silent and empty. It was not quite home anymore. Jenny vacuumed like a **fiend**, trying to get up the bucketsful of Marley fur that had been falling out in giant **clump**s for the past couple years. Slowly the signs of the old dog disappeared. One morning I went to put on my shoes, and inside them I found a layer of Marley fur. It had been picked up by my socks from walking on the floors and gradually **deposit**ed inside the shoes. I just sat and looked at it. I actually stroked it with two fingers and smiled. I held it up to show Jenny. "We're not getting rid of him that easy," I said.

She laughed, but that evening she **blurted out**, "I miss him. I mean I really, *really* miss him. I ache-inside miss him."

"I know," I said. "I do, too."

I wanted to write a farewell column to Marley, but I was afraid I would get too **mushy**. I knew I wanted to be honest. Marley was a funny, **bigger-than-life** bad boy who never did learn to obey very well. Honestly, he just might have been the world's worst-behaved dog. But

fiend ~광, 중독자 clump 뭉치, 뭉텅이 deposit 축적되다, 쌓이다 blurt out 불쑥 내뱉다 mushy 지나치게 감상적인 bigger-than-life 덩치가 산만한

he knew from the start what it meant to be man's best friend.

That weekend I took a long walk through the woods, and by the time I arrived at my newspaper office on Monday, I knew what I wanted to say about the dog that touched my life, the one I would never forget.

I began the column by describing my walk down the hill with the shovel at dawn and how odd it was to be outdoors without Marley at my side. "And now here I was alone," I wrote, "digging him this hole."

I gave a lot of thought to how I should describe him, and this is what I settled on: "No one ever called him a great dog—or even a good dog. He was as wild as a **banshee** and as strong as a bull. He **crashed** joyously **through life with a gusto** most often associated with natural disasters. As for brains, let me just say he chased his tail till the day he died, apparently convinced he **was on the verge of** a major canine **breakthrough**." But there was more to him than that. I also described his loyalty, gentleness, and his pure heart.

What I really wanted to say was how this animal had touched our souls and taught us some of the biggest

---

banshee 울어서 누군가의 죽음을 알린다는 여자 유령   crash through life 좌충우돌하는 삶을 살다
with gusto 열광적으로, 정열적으로   be on the verge of (doing) something 막 ~하려던 참이다
breakthrough 대발견, 대업적

lessons of our lives. "A person can learn a lot from a dog, even a loopy one like ours," I wrote. Marley taught me about living each day to the fullest. He taught me to **seize the moment** and follow my heart. He taught me to appreciate the simple things like a walk in the woods or a fresh snowfall. Mostly, he taught me how to be a good, loyal friend.

Was it possible for a dog—any dog, but especially a nutty, wild one like ours—to point humans to the things that really mattered in life? Things like loyalty, courage, and devotion. And the things that did not matter, too? A dog has no use for fancy cars or big homes or designer clothes. A **waterlogged** stick will do just fine. A dog judges others not by how they look but by who they are inside. A dog doesn't care if you are rich or poor, smart or dull. Give him your heart, and he will give you his. It was really quite simple.

As I wrote that farewell column to Marley, I realized it was all right there in front of us if we only opened our eyes. Sometimes it took a dog with stinky breath and bad manners to help us see what really counts in life. Despite all his flaws, Marley had given us a gift that no amount of

---

seize the moment 순간에 충실하다, 주어진 시간을 활용하다, 기회를 잡다 waterlogged 물에 젖은, 물을 흠뻑 머금은

money could buy. He gave us the gift of total, complete love. He taught us how to give it and how to accept it. When you have love, most of the other pieces fall into place.

I turned in my column, and drove home for the night, feeling somehow lighter. It was as though a weight I did not even know I had been carrying was lifted from me.

Reading Comprehension

1. Where did John dig Marley's grave?

a. under the tree where Marley liked to sleep
b. under the tree where Marley liked to poop
c. under the trees where Marley and John had the toboggan ride
d. under the tree closest to the back door

2. Which of the following was buried with Marley?

a. his dog bowl
b. pictures drawn by the children
c. Jenny's necklace
d. a photo of the family

3. Choose the correct word.

He's in a giant golden (forest/meadow), running free.
And his hips are (good/bad) again. And his (hearing/smelling) is back, and his eyesight is sharp, and he has all his (fur/teeth).

4. What kind of farewell column did John not want to write?

a. funny   b. thoughtful
c. mushy   d. loving

Answers: **1.** c **2.** b **3.** meadow, good, hearing, teeth **4.** c

24

Lucky

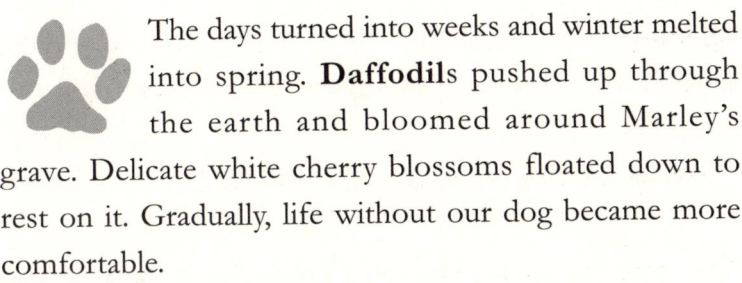

The days turned into weeks and winter melted into spring. **Daffodil**s pushed up through the earth and bloomed around Marley's grave. Delicate white cherry blossoms floated down to rest on it. Gradually, life without our dog became more comfortable.

The summer after his death, we put a swimming pool in our yard. I could not help thinking how much Marley, our tireless water dog, would have loved it. In fact, he would have loved it more than any of us possibly could.

Without a dog shedding and drooling and tracking in

daffodil 수선화

dirt, the house was a lot easier to keep clean. And I loved walking barefoot in the grass without watching for piles of poop. The garden was definitely better off without a big, heavy-pawed rabbit chaser crashing through it. No doubt about it, life without a dog was easier and much simpler. We could take a weekend trip without **arranging boarding**. We could go out to dinner without worrying what family heirloom might be destroyed. The kids could eat without having to guard their plates. The trash can did not have to go up on the kitchen counter when we left. Now we could sit back and really enjoy a good lightning storm. I especially liked the freedom of moving around the house without a giant yellow magnet glued to my heels.

Still, as a family, we were not quite whole.

One morning in late summer I came down for breakfast, and Jenny handed me a section of the newspaper folded over to show an inside page.

"You're not going to believe this," she said.

Once a week, our local paper **feature**d a dog from a rescue shelter that needed a home. The profile always

arrange 구하다, 준비하다 boarding 숙식을 제공하는 곳 feature 주요 기사로 싣다

featured a photograph of the dog, its name, and a brief description.

Staring up from the page at me was a face I instantly recognized. Our Marley. Or at least a dog that could have been his identical twin. He was a big male yellow Lab with an anvil head, **furrowed** brow and floppy ears cocked back at a comical angle. He stared directly into the camera lens with a quivering intensity that made you just know that seconds after the picture was snapped he had knocked the photographer to the ground and tried to swallow the camera. Beneath the photo, was the name—Lucky.

I read his **sales pitch** aloud. This is what Lucky had to say about himself: "**Full of zip**! I would do well in a home that is quiet while I am learning how to control my energy level. I have not had an easy life, so my new family will need to be patient with me and continue to teach me my doggie manners."

"My gosh," I exclaimed. "It's him. He's back from the dead."

"**Reincarnation**," Jenny said.

It was amazing how much Lucky looked like Marley

---

furrowed 주름이 진   sales pitch 홍보, 광고   full of zip 활력이 넘치는, 명랑한   reincarnation 환생

and how much the description fit him, too. Full of zip? Problem controlling energy? Working on doggie manners? Patience required? We knew all about these **phrase**s. They were positive ways of talking about puppy problems. We had used them ourselves.

And from the description, we knew our crazy dog was back—young and strong again, and wilder than ever. We both stood there, staring at the newspaper, not saying anything.

"I guess we could go look at him," I finally said.

"Just for the fun of it," Jenny added.

"Right. Just out of curiosity."

"**What's the harm of looking?**"

"No harm at all," I agreed.

"Well then," she said, "why not?"

"**What do we have to lose?**"

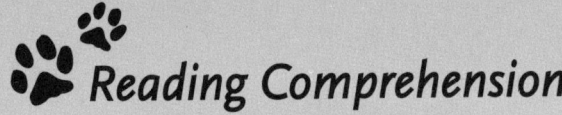# Reading Comprehension

1. Choose the correct word.

Daffodils pushed up through the (snow/earth) and bloomed around Marley's (tree/grave). Delicate white cherry blossoms floated (down/around) to rest on it. Gradually, life without our dog became more (bearable/comfortable).

2. Which was not an advantage to losing Marley?

a. The house was clean.
b. The Grogans could go on holiday without arranging boarding.
c. The Grogans could go out to dinner without worrying.
d. The Grogans felt incomplete.

3. How was Lucky different to Marley?

a. Lucky was full of zip.
b. Lucky had a different name.
c. Lucky was a different breed of dog.
d. Lucky looked different.

4. What did John and Jenny decide to do about Lucky?

a. to adopt him right away
b. to ignore him
c. to go and look at him
d. to wait and see

 1. earth, grave, down, comfortable **2.** d **3.** b **4.** c

John Grogan
Marley: A Dog Like No Other
Chapter Synopsis

Preface — The Perfect Dog

열 살이 되던 해, 나는 아버지를 졸라 강아지를 한 마리 기르게 되었다. 조그만 농장에 있는 십여 마리의 강아지 속에서 겁도 없이 깡깡대며 달려들더니 내 손가락을 핥았던 한 마리에게 한눈에 반해버렸다. 나는 그 강아지를 종이 상자에 담아 집으로 데려왔고, 이름을 숀이라고 지었다. 숀은 부모도 모르는 똥개에 불과했지만 매우 매력적인 강아지였다. 누구보다도 말을 잘 들었고, 음식은 먹으라고 할 때까진 쳐다보지도 않았다. 심지어 덤불 속에 들어가 똥을 눌 정도로 예의가 발랐다. 숀을 본 모든 사람은 저마다 칭찬을 하며 개를 키우고 싶다고 말할 정도였다. 내 어린 시절을 빛나게 한 숀은 정말 완벽한 개였다. 숀은 그 뒤로 만난 다른 개들을 판단하는 중요한 잣대가 되었다.

01. — And Puppy Makes Three

1991년 1월 어느 날, 나는 아내 제니와 함께 칠흑 같은 어둠을 뚫고 플로리다를 달렸다. 우리의 새 식구가 될 강아지를 보기 위해서였다. 꼬물거리는 새끼들 중에 한 녀석이 눈에 쏙 들어왔다. 나와 제니를 보자마자 어쩔 줄 몰라 하며 갖은 장난을 치는 녀석에게 눈길을 보내니, 주인은 기다렸다는 듯 "수컷은 375달러이지만, 특별히 350달러에 팔겠다."고 했다. 나는 겁이 없는 강아지를 고르기 위해 어릴 때부터 쓰던 방법을 시험해보기로 했다. 등을 돌렸다가 재빨리 몸을 홱 돌려 강아지들을 향해 발을 구르며 크게 소리를 질렀다. 놀라는 녀석은 없었지만, 딱 한 마리가 앞으로 펄쩍 나오며 덤벼들었다. 조금 전 그 세일 강아지였다. 우리는 이 강아지를 가족으로 받아들이고 3주 뒤에 찾으러 오기로 주인과 약속했다. 기쁜 마음으로 돌아가려는 순간 숲에서 거친 숨소리가 요란하게 났다. 그 소리는 점점 우리 쪽으로 향하더니 마침내 숲에서 튀어나와 우리 곁을 휙 지나갔다. 정신이 나가 보였지만 장난기가 가득한 눈을 가진 그것은 엄청나게 큰 래브라도 리트리버, 새끼들의 아빠였다.

02.   Homeward Bound

　3주 뒤 강아지를 데리러 다시 그곳에 간 날, 나는 경악했다. 작은 털북숭이 강아지였던 녀석이 두 배로 커져 있었기 때문이다. "집에 갈 준비됐니, 말리?" 우리 부부가 가장 좋아하는 밥 말리의 이름을 따 이미 지어놓았던 이름을 부르며 녀석을 조수석에 태웠다. 그러나 내 곁에 오려고 몸부림치는 녀석 덕분에 결국 나는 무릎 위에 말리를 앉힌 채 운전을 했다. 행복해 죽을 지경이던 말리는 핸들에다 꼬리를 일정한 간격으로 쳤다. 내 손가락이 자기 머리에 닿는 개수가 늘어갈수록 꼬리가 핸들을 치는 속도는 더욱 빨라졌다. 집에 도착하자 말리는 킁킁거리며 집안 구경을 하고는 털썩 주저앉아 나를 빤히 바라보았다. 형과 누나와 동생을 찾는 눈치였다. 나는 차고에 마련해 놓은 집에 말리를 데려다 놓았다. 머리를 쓰다듬어주고 차고에서 나오자 말리는 울부짖기 시작했다. 그렇게 하기를 몇 번, 나는 결국 말리를 데리고 나와 침실에서 함께 잘 수밖에 없었다. 녀석이 숨을 쉴 때마다 갈비뼈가 오르락내리락했다. 우리 둘은 그제야 꿈나라로 빠져들었다.

03.   Mr. Wiggles

　날이 갈수록 녀석의 기운은 천하장사가 되었다. 집안에 남아나는 물건이 없을 정도였다. 말리는 밥을 주기가 무섭게 부스러기 하나 남기지 않고 밥그릇을 비웠고, 똥도 엄청나게 많이 쌌다. 그리고 무서운 속도로 자랐다. 꼬리의 힘은 또 얼마나 센지 거침없이 휘두르는 꼬리 때문에 작은 탁자가 넘어지고 잡지들은 사방으로 흩어졌으며 병과 컵이 공중으로 날아다녔다. 꼬리뿐만이 아니었다. 뭔가를 입에 물었을 때는 온몸을 뒤흔들었다. 우리는 그 녀석을 몸부림 챔피언이라 불렀다. 작은 물건을 입안에 숨겨놓고 장난치는 것을 좋아했다. 녀석을 코너로 몰아 입안을 벌려 살펴보면, 종이 타월, 식료품 영수증, 포도주 마개, 병뚜껑 등등 고물상 주인처럼 많은 물건이 쏟아져 나왔다. "얘는 사는 게 즐거운가 보네요." 누군가가 말했다. 신나는 놀이동산에 온 것처럼 삶을 사는 말리를 우리는 더욱 사랑할 수밖에 없었다.

04. Master and Beast

말리는 쑥쑥 자랐다. 녀석을 처음 본 수의사마저 휘파람을 불며 "엄청나게 크겠는데."라고 말할 정도였으니까. 현관문에 난 작은 유리창 너머로 밖을 볼 수 있을 만큼 자란 말리는 손님이 오는 것을 무척 좋아했다. 초인종이 울리면 가장 먼저 달려나가 현관문 앞에서 신나게 짖어대 바깥에 서 있던 사람들이 놀라 도망칠 정도였다. 어느 날 아침, 나는 제니와 함께 말리를 데리고 수영을 하러 갔다. 해변에서 막대기를 힘껏 던져 다시 가져오게 하는 방법을 가르쳐 주었다. 물건을 가져오려는 본능을 지닌 래브라도 리트리버 종답게 말리는 던진 막대기를 신나게 쫓아갔다. 하지만 녀석에겐 막대기를 내게 돌려주려는 마음은 전혀 없어 보였다.  나는 말리를 길들이려고 새 막대기를 꺼냈다. 어떻게 하면 입에 물고 있는 것을 뺏기지 않으면서 새 막대기를 가질 수 있을까, 망설이는 눈빛이 역력했다. 몇 번을 연습시키고 나서야 말리는 조금씩 알아갔다. 받으려면 줄 줄 알아야 한다는 것을.

05. A Battle of Wills

말리가 6개월쯤 되었을 때, 우리는 말리를 훈련소로 데려가기로 결정했다. 해변에서 막대기를 물어오는 것 외엔 할 줄 아는 게 아무것도 없었다. 훈련소로 데리고 간 날, 말리는 어김없이 다른 강아지들의 꽁무니를 쫓아다니느라 여념이 없었고, 깐깐한 조련사는 말리를 탐탁지 않게 여겼다. 개는 오직 한 주인만을 섬긴다는 조련사 말에 어쩔 수 없이 제니가 훈련에 동참했지만, 온종일 말리에게 끌려 다니느라 제니가 훈련을 받는 건지 말리가 받는 건지 모를 정도였다. 다음번엔 조련사가 직접 나섰다. 말리는 조련사를 골탕먹이듯 조련사를 끌고 다녔고, 나는 나름 통쾌한 기분을 느꼈다. 많은 사람 앞에서 망신을 당했다고 생각한 조련사는 말리와 나를 내쫓았고, 이에 자극을 받은 나는 집에서 열심히 말리를 훈련시켰다. 훈련에 성공한 날, 말리를 두고 집을 비웠는데 마침 심한 천둥 번개로 놀란 말리는 차고 곳곳을 부수는 사고를 저지르고 말았다.

06. The Great Escape

말썽꾸러기는 말리 하나로 충분했기에 우리는 말리가 아빠가 되는 것을 원치 않았다. 동물 병원에 데리고 가기로 한 날, 뒷좌석에 탔던 말리는 제니가 브레이크를 밟을 때마다 유리창에 코를 박았지만, 세상에서 가장 친한 두 사람과 하는 드라이브의 행복감에 깊이 젖어 있었다. 어느새 내 무릎에 앉아 바깥 구경을 하고 있는 말리를 위해서 나는 창문을 조금 열어주었다. 말리는 창문 밖으로 고개를 쑥 내밀고는 바람에 귀를 펄럭거리며 행복해했다. 제니가 말리가 신경쓰인다고 말하는 순간, 갑자기 녀석의 앞다리가 창밖으로 주르르 미끄러졌다. 손 쓸 겨를도 없이 달리는 차 밖으로 뛰어나가려고 몸부림을 쳤고, 놀란 제니는 달리는 도로에서 급브레이크를 밟았다. 겨우 꼬리만을 잡고 버티고 있던 나 대신에 제니가 운전석에서 내려 말리의 목줄을 잡았고, 그제야 겨우 다시 말리를 차 안으로 들일 수 있었다. 도로 한복판에서 벌인 쇼로 인해 구경꾼들은 배를 잡고 웃었다.

07. The Things He Ate

제니의 출산 날이 다가올수록 우리는 말리를 훈련시키는 일에 박차를 가했다. 말리는 눈앞에 새로운 것이 나타나지 않을 때만큼은 말을 잘 들었다. 문제는 그 새로운 것이 너무 자주 나타난다는 거다. 말리는 닥치는 대로 먹어치웠다. 그래서 말리의 커다란 똥 무덤은 여기저기 널려 있었다. 망고로 배를 채운 날은 밝은 오렌지색 똥이, 냅킨을 먹은 날은 파란색 똥이 가득했다. 똥을 자세히 살펴보면 말리가 무엇을 먹었는지 알 수 있다. 고무줄, 사이다 병뚜껑, 빗, 심지어 볼펜뚜껑까지 나온 적이 있다. 어느 날, 맘보춤을 추며 걸어오는 말리의 입에 반짝이는 줄이 보였다. 설마! 그건 제니에게 생일선물로 준 금목걸이였다. 갖은 노력을 했지만 목걸이는 말리의 목구멍으로 빨려 들어갔다. 우리는 한동안 말리의 똥을 탐색하는 수밖에 없었다. 금목걸이는 다행히 찾아냈다. 제니는 그걸 어디서 찾아냈는지 개의치 않았다.

08.   The Dog's Got to Go

우리는 다섯 식구가 되었다. 나와 제니, 말리 그리고 두 아들 녀석. 장난꾸러기가 두 명이나 더 늘자, 제니는 몹시 힘겨워했다. 말리가 소파를 뜯어먹은 날 제니는 폭발하고 말았다. 말리를 때리기 시작했다. 내가 말리자 제니는 울면서 말리를 내보내라고 말했다. 나는 말리를 데리고 나가 훈련을 시키며 제니의 화가 풀릴 때까지 거리를 배회했다. 하지만 제니는 단호했다. "말리를 내보내." 나는 말리를 데리고 개 훈련소를 다시 찾았다. 처음에 갔던 조련사와는 사뭇 달랐다. 말리도 전보다 말썽이 줄었다. 8주간의 훈련이 끝나고 드디어 시험 날. 나는 말리에게 가르친 갖가지 것들을 조련사 앞에서 보였다. 그날 저녁, 조련사는 우리에게 수료증을 주었다. 말리는 반에서 7등으로 기본 복종훈련을 통과했다. 반 학생은 전부 여덟 명이었고, 8등은 정신 나간 핏불 테리어였지만 이정도면 충분했다. 나는 사실 녀석이 수료증만 씹어대지 않았더라면 눈물을 흘릴 뻔했다.

09.   The Final Round

말리와 나 사이에는 매듭을 짓지 못한 문제가 남아 있었다. 사람들에게 뛰어올라 매달리는 버릇을 고쳐야 했다. 어떤 사람이 "정말로 녀석의 버릇을 고쳐주고 싶다면 개가 뛰어오를 때 무릎으로 녀석의 가슴을 올려 쳐라."고 말했다. 처음엔 너무 심하다고 생각했지만 한번 실험해보기로 했다. 말리가 나를 향해 전속력으로 다가와 뛰어올랐을 때, 나는 눈을 꼭 감고 녀석의 갈비뼈 아래 푹신한 부분을 무릎으로 쳤다. 헉! 말리는 바닥으로 미끄러졌고, 곧 상처받은 얼굴로 나를 바라봤다. 녀석에게 미안했지만 어쩔 수 없었다. 다음에도 그다음에도 나는 계속 녀석이 뛰어오르면 무릎으로 쳤다. 사흘째 되던 날, 말리는 마침내 버릇을 고쳤다. 그러나 나를 제외한 다른 사람에게는 여전했다. 나는 친구에게 부탁해 그 방법을 써 달라고 했다. 말리는 그 친구에게 혹을 당하고 난 뒤의 충격으로 다시는 사람들에게 펄쩍 뛰어오르지 않았다. 아, 좋은 소식 하나! 제니는 다시 말리를 사랑하기 시작했다.

10. The Audition

제니가 전화를 걸어 말리가 영화 오디션을 보게 되었다고 했을 때, 나는 순간 귀를 의심했다. "말리가 무엇을 한다고?" 자초지종을 들으니, 뉴욕 영화사 관계자가 일반 가정집 자료 조사를 하던 중, 우리 집에 와서 말리를 본 것이다. 때마침 크고 정신없고 설치는 개가 필요했다며 말리를 매우 좋아했다는 것이다. 말리는 결국 오디션에 통과해 촬영을 하게 됐다. 그날의 촬영은 차가 갓길에 서면 문이 열리면서 꼬마 아이가 목줄에 묶인 말리를 데리고 내리는 장면이었다. 식은 죽 먹기라고 생각했다. 그러나 총알 같이 뛰어나가 NG, 목줄을 끊어버려 NG, 말리 녀석 때문에 아이가 겁에 질린 표정을 지어 NG, 결국 장면은 OK를 받지 못했다. 그것 말고도 배우 의상을 침으로 세탁한다든가, 간식 상을 뒤엎어 버린다든가 하는 각종 사고에 "우리가 전화할 때까지 절대 오지 마라."는 통보를 들어야 했다.

11. Take Two

다음 날 아침, 전화가 왔다. 말리를 데리고 호텔로 오라는 것이다. "말리를 다시 쓰겠다고요?" 우리는 서둘러 촬영장에 도착했다. 감독은 어제 촬영한 필름원본을 보고 무척이나 마음에 들어했다. "물불을 가리지 않는 진정한 천재"라나? 촬영은 며칠 동안 계속되었고, 어제와는 달리 말리는 왕 대접을 받았다. 사람들이 물시중, 간식 시중을 들었다. 나는 으쓱했다. 우리는 꼬박 나흘 동안 촬영장에 있었고, 말리가 출연한 영화를 본 건 그로부터 2년이 지난 뒤였다. 비디오 가게에서 단 한 명도 빌려보지 않은 〈마지막 홈런〉을 들고 와 가족과 함께 보았다. 말리는 딱 2분 동안 화면에 등장했다. 하지만 그 2분이 그 영화에서 가장 재미있었다. 우리는 배꼽을 잡고 울고 웃었다. 정작 말리는 하품을 하며 잠이 들었지만. 영화가 끝나고 우리는 숨을 죽이며 출연자 명단을 기다렸다. 순간 이름을 빼먹지 않았을까 의심도 했지만 곧 커다란 글씨가 화면에 나타났다. 말리(말리 역).

12.   Jail Break

우리는 보카 라톤에 있는 좀 더 큰 집으로 이사했다. 새집은 공원 옆에 있는 수영장이 딸린 좋은 집이었다. 말리보다 수영장을 더 좋아한 사람은 아무도 없었다. 말리는 모든 것을 마음에 들어 했다. 아쉬운 게 있다면, 새집에는 말리가 부술 수 없을 만큼 튼튼한 요새가 없다는 점이었다. 새로 이사한 집 차고에 말리를 가둬놓기엔 숨이 턱턱 막힐 정도로 더웠다. 우리는 외출할 때마다 부엌 옆 세탁실에 말리를 가둬두었다. 천둥 번개가 치기 전까진 그럭저럭 괜찮았다. 먹구름이 몰려와 우리는 서둘러 집으로 돌아왔지만, 때는 이미 늦었다. 말리는 피투성이가 된 채 그 튼튼한 세탁실 벽을 뚫어놓았다. 우리는 대책을 세웠다. 아무도 열 수 없을 것 같은 튼튼한 강철 우리를 마련했다. 그러나 그날 저녁 말리는 우리를 탈출했고, 얼마 안 가 강철 우리는 찌그러진 고철 덩어리가 되어버렸다.

13.   Dinner Time!

비싼 몸값을 자랑하는 세련되고 작은 개들이 넘쳐나는 보카 라톤에서 말리는 마치 발레 무용수들 틈에 낀 스모 선수 같았다. 문제는 말리가 그런 개들을 보면 좋아서 무작정 덤벼든다는 데 있었다. 말리에게 눈길조차 주지 않는 개들에게 목줄이 끊길 정도로 달려가는 말리. 그런 말리 때문에 우리는 당혹스러웠던 적이 한두 번이 아니었다. 어느 날은 온 식구가 근사한 식당의 야외 테이블에서 식사를 하기로 했다. 야외 테이블 다리에 말리의 목줄을 묶고 이 멋진 날을 위해 건배하려는 순간, 테이블이 움직이기 시작했다. 콧대 높은 푸들과 그의 주인을 본 말리가 마침내 테이블을 끌고 그들을 향하여 달려갔다. 소동이 있은 후 나는 '그래도 말리는 똥을 먹진 않잖아'라며 스스로를 위안했다. 그러나 그런 위안도 잠시, 말리는 고양이의 용변 상자에 가득 든 똥을 쟁취한 후 최고로 행복한 표정을 지었다.

14. Lightning Strikes

제니와 나 사이에는 뒤늦게 딸아이가 생겼다. 콜린이 태어난 지 일주일이 지났을 때 우리는 아기를 데리고 처음 바깥으로 나갔다. 나는 두 아들과 함께 앞마당에 꽃을 심고 있었고, 말리는 나무 그늘 아래 누워 세상 돌아가는 풍경을 구경했다. 제니는 콜린이 누워 있는 요람을 말리 옆 풀밭에 놓았다. 아이들이 심어놓은 꽃을 구경하라고 제니를 불렀다. 우리는 줄지어 선 큰 나무들 뒤로 들어갔다. 그곳에서 우리는 낮잠을 자는 콜린을 볼 수 있었지만 거리 쪽에서는 우리가 보이지 않았다. 집 앞을 지나가던 한 노부부가 우리 집 앞마당에 펼쳐진 광경을 보고는 눈이 휘둥그레져서 걸음을 멈추었다. 커다란 누렁이 개 혼자서 갓난아이를 돌보는 것처럼 보였기 때문이다. 신고를 해야 하나 잔뜩 놀란 노부부를 위해 우리는 다시 나무를 빠져나와 손을 흔들어 주었다. 그리고 얼마 뒤 말리와 함께 정원에 나와 있을 때 강력한 천둥 번개가 쳤다. 나 역시 말리처럼 공포를 느꼈다. 말리의 공포를 이해한 나는 다시는 말리의 두려움을 무시하지 않겠다고 마음먹었다.

15. Dog Beach

나는 말리와 함께 도그 비치로 갔다. 플로리다의 도그 비치는 개들과 개 주인이 마음 놓고 놀 수 있도록 허용된 모래사장이었다. 규칙은 사나운 개들은 목줄을 채워야 하고, 개 주인들은 비닐봉지를 가져와서 이들이 싼 똥과 쓰레기를 모두 치워야 하며, 절대 물속에서 일을 봐서는 안 된다는 것이었다. 말리를 데려간 그날은 경찰이 다녀가 모든 개에게 목줄을 채워야 한다는 규칙으로 바뀐 날이었다.

그러나 해변이 눈앞에 있는데 말리에게 목줄을 채워야 한다는 것은 나에게도 곤욕이었다. 그래서 어쩔 수 없이 불안하지만 말리를 풀어 해변으로 보냈다. 순식간에 파도 속으로 사라진 말리는 다른 개들과 장난을 치며 즐겁게 놀았다. 그러나 얼마 후 짠물을 잔뜩 들이킨 말리는 몸을 뒤틀더니 토하기 시작했다. 나는 얼른 가서 녀석의 토사물을 치워야 했다. 그리고 겨우 한숨 돌리려는 순간, 녀석은 물속에서 똥을 쌌다. 다시는 이 녀석을 해변으로 데려오지 않으리라 마음먹은 순간이었다.

16. A Northbound Plane

펜실베이니아에 새 일자리를 얻어서 우리는 그동안 살던 집을 팔고 플로리다를 떠나게 됐다. 비행기를 타려고 공항으로 갔다. 우리는 말리를 우리 안에 넣어 짐칸에 실어야 했다. 항공사 카운터에서 말리와 우리를 보더니, 말리가 들어가기엔 우리가 너무 작다고 했다. 애완용품점에서 가장 큰 우리를 산 것이기 때문에 더 이상의 방법이 없으니. 억지로 말리를 집어넣어 일단 우리 안에 말리가 들어가는 것을 보여주었다. 우리가 보기에도 비좁아 보였다. 그러나 어쩔 수 없었다. 우리는 막무가내로 항공사 직원을 설득하여 말리를 비행기 짐칸에 겨우 실을 수 있었다. 이륙을 준비하기 위해 비행기가 엔진을 켰고, 나는 잡지를 펼쳐들었다. 갑자기 제니가 얼어붙었다. 내 귀에도 소리가 들려왔다. 우리 발밑, 비행기의 어디선가 나는 늑대처럼 울부짖는 소리. 말리가 저 아래서 울부짖고 있었다. 승무원들도 승객들도 고개를 갸웃하며 소리에 귀 기울이기 시작했다. 우리는 모른 척할 수밖에 없었다. 하지만 가는 내내 말리가 걱정되었다.

17. In the Land of Pencils

펜실베이니아에 온 우리는 넓은 마당과 숲이 딸린 큰 집으로 이사했다. 코너는 펜실베이니아에 펜슬(연필)이 많지 않다며 눈물을 흘렸다. 아이들과 말리는 시골 생활에 잘 적응하기 시작했다. 채소 도둑인 토끼를 잡으려고 노력하기도 했고, 잔뜩 쌓아 놓은 낙엽 위로 풀썩 주저앉는 놀이도 좋아했다. 태어나서 한 번도 눈을 본 적 없는 아이들과 말리는 온 세상이 하얗게 덮인 함박눈 풍경도 경험했다. 말리는 처음엔 무척 낯설어하더니 나중에는 개답게 온 사방에 눈발자국을 찍어 놓았다. 나는 눈썰매를 타고 싶었다. 출발하는 순간 내 배 위로 탑승한 말리와 함께 신나게 눈썰매를 탔다. 문득 말리와 함께 한 시간이 벌써 9년이 지났음을 깨달았다. 예전에 비해 굼뜨긴 했지만 장난은 여전한 말리. 그 녀석이 사고 친 일로 수리한 비용은 요트 한 척에 달하지만, 요트보다 훨씬 더 재미있는 일들을 우리에게 많이 안겨주었다.

18. Poultry on Parade

우리는 이곳에서 가축을 키워보기로 했다. 제니와 나는 어떤 동물을 키울 것인지 대책 회의를 한 후 닭을 키우기로 결정했다. 제니의 친구에게서 병아리 몇 마리를 얻어왔다. 한 농장 주인은 우리에게 한 가지를 당부했다. "아이들이 닭 이름을 짓지 못하게 해야 해요. 한번 이름을 지으면 그것은 애완동물이지, 가축이 아니에요." 말이 떨어지기가 무섭게 아이들은 "내 병아리는 깃털", "내 병아리는 뽀송이", "내 병아리는 짹짹이"라고 이름을 지었다. 깃털과 뽀송이, 짹짹이, 셜리는 우리와 함께 살기 시작했다. 몇 주가 지나서야, 네 마리 중 세 마리가 알은 못 낳고 시끄럽기만 한 수탉임이 밝혀졌다. 집 안은 점점 시끄러워졌다. 그런데도 말리는 잠을 잘 잤다. 그제서야 난 말리가 거의 귀머거리가 되어간다는 사실을 깨달았다. 녀석은 잘 못 듣고, 점점 행동이 굼떠졌지만 먹성만은 여전했다.

19. The Potty Room

사람이 한 살을 먹는 동안 개들은 일곱 살을 먹는다. 이제 말리는 아흔 살을 바라보는 할아버지 개가 되었다. 이빨은 갈색으로 변했고, 입 냄새는 고약해졌다. 소화력도 저하되어 방귀대장이 되었다. 냄새는 어찌나 지독한지, 방귀를 한번 뀌면 우리는 모두 도망가야 할 지경이 되었다. 가끔 사라지기도 했다. 능글맞게 어슬렁어슬렁 멀리 가버려서 가끔 제니와 나는 말리를 찾는 데 온 시간을 소비했다. 지쳐서 집에 가면 말리는 집 앞 현관에 와 있어 우리를 화나게 하기도 했다. 말리는 눈도 흐려졌다. 토끼들이 몇 발짝 앞에서 알짱거리는데도 알아차리지 못했다. 가장 걱정스러웠던 것은 엉덩이였다. 말리는 관절염 때문에 고생하고 있었다. 그런데도 우리를 발견하면 2층으로 힘겹게 올라왔고, 내가 1층으로 내려오면 기어코 따라 내려왔다. 계단 오르기 챔피언이었던 녀석이 고작 두 계단을 못 오르고 한참을 망설이는 모습을 나는 씁쓸하게 지켜봐야 했다.

20. Beating the Odds

여름 방학을 맞아 말리를 애견 훈련소에 잠깐 맡겼다. 훈련소에 맡긴 내내 마음이 편하지 않았다. 그러던 어느 날, 수의사에게서 전화가 왔다. 말리의 위가 거꾸로 뒤집히면서 꼬이는 바람에 뱃속에 든 음식과 물과 공기가 한데 엉켜버려 목숨이 위태로운 지경까지 갔었다고 했다. 다시 위가 꼬일 확률은 99퍼센트라고 했다. 수술은 늙은 말리에겐 굉장히 위험했고, 수술을 하지 않을 경우엔 말리를 위해 안락사하는 방법이 있다고 했다. 우리는 1퍼센트에 희망을 걸기로 했고, 다행히 말리는 조금씩 차도를 보이기 시작했다. 말리를 데려온 날 밤, 나는 거실 바닥에 침낭을 펴고 말리와 함께 잤다. 지난 13년간의 시간이 내 머릿속을 스쳐갔다. 말리는 오랫동안 충직하고 좋은 벗이었다. 나는 옆에 붙어 있는 말리에게 속삭였다. "너 때문에 간 떨어지는 줄 알았다. 이 영감탱이야."

21. Borrowed Time

말리는 죽음의 문턱에서 살아 돌아왔다. 녀석의 눈에 다시 반짝이는 장난기가 돌았고 약간이긴 했지만 살도 붙었다. 식탐은 더 늘어나 전보다 심하게 밥 달라고 졸랐고, 더 뻔뻔하게 음식을 훔쳐 먹었다. 음식을 먹겠다는 의지 하나로 약한 뒷다리로 섰을 때는 너무 기특해서 꽉 안아주고 싶었다. 취재차 떠난 출장길에 집으로 전화했더니, 제니는 말리가 나를 너무 보고 싶어 한다고 전했다. 출장을 마치고 집으로 돌아온 지 일주일 되던 날, 말리는 계단에서 떨어졌다. 다행히 뼈는 부러지지 않았지만 힘줄이 늘어났는지 깽깽대고 몹시 힘들어했다. 늘 누던 자리에서 오줌 누는 습관 때문에 말리는 10시간 이상 오줌을 참았다. 나는 말리를 들어 세워 현관으로 나갔다. 이후 우리는 배변을 위해 말리를 들어 현관으로 옮겨야 했다. 그런데 말리의 죽음을 맞을 마음의 준비를 해야겠다고 생각한 다음날 말리는 나를 찾아 2층으로 힘겹게 올라왔다. 나는 감격해서 말리를 꼭 껴안으며 칭찬해 주었다.

22. The Big Meadow

나는 말리가 이번 겨울을 넘길 수 있을까 걱정이 되었다. 어느 추운 밤, 제니가 다같이 집에서 영화를 보자고 했다. 나는 거실에 장작을 피우고 아이들은 비디오테이프를 틀었다. 베개를 베고 누워 있는 무방비 상태의 나를 보는 말리의 표정은 여전히 장난기가 감돌았다. 뒤뚱뒤뚱 걸어와 나를 짓눌렀다. 나는 이런 날이 또 오지 않을 거란 생각에 바닥에 깔린 채 말리의 기분을 좋게 해주었다. 일주일간 동물병원에 말리를 맡긴 채 우리 가족은 디즈니랜드에서 놀다 왔다. 말리는 전보다 엉덩이가 더 굳어 있었고 정신이 몽롱해 보였다. 그리고 자꾸 토하려 하면서 바닥에 축 늘어졌다. 녀석의 배는 두 배로 부풀어 있었다. 다시 위가 뒤집혀 있다는 것을 알 수 있었다. 이제 정말 말리의 마지막을 준비해야 했다. 심장이 멎은 말리를 동물병원에서 데리고 오는 동안 눈물이 멈추지 않았다.

23. Beneath the Cherry Trees

말리를 떠나보내고 나는 잠을 이루지 못한 채 뒤척이다가 동트기 한 시간 전에 자리에서 일어났다. 나는 눈 오던 날, 말리와 함께 신나게 눈썰매를 탔던 숲의 벚나무 아래 말리의 무덤을 만들고 녀석을 묻었다. 그리고 가족을 데리고 왔다. "말리, 우리는 너를 사랑해." 미리 연습이나 한 것처럼 아내와 아이들은 눈물을 흘리며 동시에 말했다. 말리를 묻고 나서 한동안 아무도 말리에 대해 이야기하지 않았다. 제니는 미친 듯이 진공청소기를 돌려 말리의 털을 한 양동이씩 치웠다. 2,3년 동안 빠진 털이 뭉텅이로 나왔다. 어느 날 아침엔 신발을 신는데 말리의 털이 뭉쳐 나왔다. "우리 말리가 이렇게 쉽게 물러날 리 없지." 우스갯소리에 제니는 말리가 너무 보고 싶어 가슴이 아프다고 말했다. 나는 말리에 대한 칼럼을 쓰기 시작했다. 정직하게 최선을 다해 쓴 칼럼을 완성하고 나니 그간 가슴을 짓누르던 바윗덩어리가 떨어져 나간 기분이었다.

24.   Lucky

우리는 말리 없이 살아가는 삶에 조금씩 익숙해졌다. 집은 전보다 깨끗해졌고, 아이들은 제 음식을 빼앗기지 않으려 접시를 가리지 않아도 되었다. 특히 나는 뒤꿈치에 딱 붙어 졸졸 따라다니는 거대한 누렁이 없이 집 안을 마음껏 돌아다니는 자유를 누렸다. 하지만 어딘가 허전한 기운을 완전히 떨치지는 못했다. 어느 날 제니가 신문을 건네며 "믿지 못할 일이 발생했다."고 말했다. 유기견 보호소의 광고란엔 놀랍게도 말리의 얼굴이 있었다. 사진 밑에는 "이름: 럭키/자기소개: 성격이 좀 팔팔함"이라고 적혀 있었다. 말리가 환생한 것이다. "이 녀석을 만나러 가볼까 봐." 내가 먼저 말을 꺼냈다. 제니 역시 "그래. 그냥 재미 삼아 가보자고."라며 맞장구를 쳤다.